The Power of Solitude

Marion Yorck von Wartenburg

The Power of Solitude

My Life in the German Resistance

Translated and edited by Julie M. Winter

With an introduction by Peter Hoffmann

University of Nebraska Press: Lincoln & London

Originally published as *Die Stärke der Stille: Erzählung eines Lebens aus dem deutschen Widerstand*, © 1984 Eugen Diederichs Verlag GmbH & Co. KG, Köln Original narration recorded by Claudia Schmölders Translation and introduction © 2000 by the University of Nebraska Press. All rights reserved. Manufactured in the United States of America ∞

Library of Congress Cataloging-in-Publication Data
Yorck von Wartenburg, Marion, 1904–
[Stärke der Stille. English]
The power of solitude : my life in the German resistance / Marion Yorck von Wartenburg ; translated and edited by Julie M. Winter ; with an introduction by Peter Hoffman.
p. cm. "Original narration recorded by Claudia Schmölders" – T.p. verso. ISBN 0-8032-4915-2 (cl.: alkaline paper). — ISBN 0-8032-9915-x (pbk : alkaline paper) 1. Yorck von Wartenburg, Marion, 1904– . 2. Anti-Nazi movement— Germany Biography. 3. Hitler, Adolf, 1889–1945 — Assassination attempt, 1944 (July 20) I. Winter, Julie M., 1957– . II. Schmölders, Claudia. III. Title.
DD256.3.Y67 2000
943.086′092—dc21 [B] 99-42656 CIP

In memory of Peter on his eightieth birthday, 13 November 1984

Contents

Translator's Note

THE FOLLOWING is a translation of an oral autobiographical account of the life of Marion Yorck von Wartenburg. Marion Yorck was involved in the Nazi resistance group known as the Kreisau Circle, whose cofounder was her husband, Peter. The Kreisau Circle participated in the assassination attempt on Adolf Hitler on 20 July 1944, which was carried out by Col. Claus Stauffenberg—a cousin of Peter Yorck's—and other members of the military resistance. The Kreisau group was to be active in the government takeover after the death of Hitler. When the attempt failed, hundreds of people were arrested, tried, and executed, including Peter Yorck. Marion Yorck and hundreds of family members of the conspirators were also arrested and spent months in jail in miserable conditions.

In this lively and poignant memoir, originally published in West Germany in 1984, Marion Yorck describes these events, as well as her life before she married and after her husband's execution. Born in Berlin in 1904, Marion Yorck studied law there and completed her doctorate in 1929. In 1930 she married Peter Count Yorck von Wartenburg and spent her early years of marriage in Berlin, Breslau, and at the Yorck family estate of Kauern. She was warmly received by her husband's family, and she in turn developed a deep affection for them and for their Silesian homeland. At her husband's side she witnessed and participated in the resistance against Hitler. After the war Marion Yorck returned to the law profession; she passed her licensing exam and soon became a judge in a local court in West Berlin. In 1952 she became the first woman in Germany to preside over a jury court. Until 1969 she also presided over a grand juvenile court.

Claudia Schmölders compiled the original German book from extended interview records. Marion Yorck carefully examined and approved of the text. Her language is rich with flavoring words that add a certain emphasis to her sentences, and these cannot always be accurately rendered into English. In cases where they could not be translated, I have attempted to convey their particular emphasis in the context of the whole passage.

Often Marion Yorck's speech trails off, indicated in the text by ellipses. The brackets used in Peter Yorck's letters to his wife at the end of this memoir indicate explanations by Marion Yorck in the original German. I have used footnotes on occasion to clarify certain phrases or issues, and I have supplied a glossary of German terms and names at the end of the work.

I would like to thank Ruth Schwertfeger for encouraging me to translate this book. Marion Yorck's story has moved me profoundly, and I am very grateful for this experience. My greatest debt goes to Herbert Winter, who read the manuscript to ensure accuracy and who came up with many wonderful English renderings of difficult German phrases. I also want to thank Helen Winter, who made sure the English version flowed. Torie Fechner of Berlin, Germany, shared her German language expertise and her intimate knowledge of Berlin many times, and I am very grateful to her. Thank you also to Gregory Winter, my husband—and my best critic and editor. My children, Conrad and Christoph, also helped by reminding me at times what we really say in English. This translation would not have been possible without the help and support of all these people.

JULIE M. WINTER

Introduction

MARION YORCK's thoughtful memoir provides a view of a part of German society that rejected National Socialism and the war at a time when resistance to the regime was considered treason. The resisters regarded the war as a crime against humanity, and they saw that their own government was committing millionfold crimes against Jews, other minorities, Poles, soldiers and civilians of the Soviet Union, and numerous other nations under German military occupation. An outline of external events will place the narrative in its historical context.

The right to resist an authority that acts without legitimacy has a long tradition in European thought. In the nineteenth century, an age of the ascendancy of the state as the superior form of human organization, the concept of a right to resist became displaced by loyalty to authority and by nationalism. But the ideas of natural law and inalienable rights were still alive.

The constitutional procedures of government in Germany had been under attack since a German republic had come into existence in 1918. The constitutional foundations of the republic were fatally weakened during the economic collapse of the Great Depression between 1929 and 1933, amid mass unemployment and the failure of the democratic parties to agree on a working government. President Paul von Hindenburg was forced to appoint governments under his own authority, without parliamentary backing, according to article 48 of the Constitution. The eighty-four-year-old president had wished to retire at the end of his seven-year term in 1932, but he had been persuaded to stand once again in order to prevent the election of Adolf Hitler.

During the years 1930–32 the National Socialists gained large voting successes, partly because the first "presidential" chancellor, Heinrich Brüning, called early elections in order to win a mandate from the voters for austerity measures. He did this at what turned out to be a most inopportune moment. Hitler's party, the National Socialist German Workers' Party, having languished for years at just above 2 percent of votes cast in national elections, won 18.3 percent of the vote in September 1930, and in the next national parliamentary election in July 1932, with voter participation above 80 percent, the party increased its share to 37.4 percent. But it was not enough. The National Socialists never came close to winning a majority of votes, and propaganda chief Joseph Goebbels expressed his frustration: "Something must happen. . . . We won't get to an absolute majority this way."[1]

In several weeks of intense behind-the-scenes intrigues, in December 1932 and in January 1933, however, President von Hindenburg was persuaded by a handful of unofficial advisers that Hitler could form a coalition cabinet based on a parliamentary majority, and thus restore government stability on the basis of the Constitution, and that this would end the months of near civil war.[2] The cabinet President von Hindenburg appointed on 30 January 1933 included the National Socialists Adolf Hitler (chancellor), Wilhelm Frick (interior), Hermann Göring (without portfolio); the former Center Party politician, now without party affiliation Franz von Papen (vice-chancellor); the National-Socialist sympathizer without party affiliation Werner von Blomberg (war); the politicians without party affiliation Konstantin Baron von Neurath (foreign affairs), Johann Ludwig Count Schwerin von Krosigk (finance), Paul Baron Eltz von Rübenach (post, transport); the Stahlhelm veterans' legion leader Franz Seldte (labor); the German National People's Party leader Alfred Hugenberg (economics, food), and the German National People's Party politician Franz Gürtner (justice).

Hitler, of course, did not at all plan to restore constitutional and government stability. The first item on his agenda was to use all available means, both legal and illegal, to consolidate his power and to secure it against any future challenge from the parliament, the president, the military leaders, the trade unions, the churches, or the voters.

Hermann Göring, one of Hitler's closest associates and now the Prussian interior minister (soon also Prussian minister president, and thus in direct control of approximately two-thirds of Germany), left no room for doubt that the National Socialists meant to have absolute power. On 17 February 1933 he ordered the Prussian police to use their firearms in any encounters with "enemies" of the new national state and threatened disciplinary procedures against policemen who were "inappropriately considerate." Göring's decree was published on the front page of the Party newspaper, *Völkischer Beobachter*, on 21 February 1933. The world was on notice that shootings by the police were carried out under government orders. Emergency decrees for the "protection of people and state" suspended the civil rights of all Germans and gave the government emergency authority, unchecked by parliamentary controls. On 5 March 1933, after four weeks of National Socialist terror in the streets, after thousands had been imprisoned in concentration camps and hundreds had been shot or beaten to death, and amid widespread intimidation of voters by the SA, 56 percent still did not vote for the National Socialists. The National Socialists in the Reichstag moved an enabling bill that was to give them dictatorial powers. The Social Democratic faction voted against it. The bill nevertheless passed with the necessary two-thirds majority only because the Catholic Center Party supported it (in view of concordat negotiations with the Vatican). Special courts (*Sondergerichte*) were now set up with almost unlimited jurisdiction and without the possibility of appeal.

Hitler's propaganda presented the German nation as in overwhelming support of the National Socialist regime. But the British ambassador in Berlin, Sir Eric Phipps, reported in 1934 that the German people had been deprived of their liberty, and that any action they might take in opposition to the government was regarded as high treason and was punishable by death.[3] The German people were free to cheer but not free to criticize.

Open opposition was soon outlawed and gradually destroyed by the police. Communists and socialists were rendered ineffective as organized sources of opposition, although numerous individuals carried out acts of defiance, resistance, and sabotage against the Nazi regime.

In 1936 the Secret State Police, called the Gestapo, seized 1,643,200 underground propaganda leaflets distributed mostly by Social Democrats and Communists, and 927,430 in 1937. Between 1933 and 1945, tens of thousands of Germans were murdered in camps and penitentiaries. From 1933 to 1945, *Sondergerichte* killed 12,000 Germans;[4] "regular" German justice killed 40,000 Germans; courts-martial killed 25,000 German soldiers (western Allied courts-martial killed under 300 during the Second World War). The total of Germans killed through judicial processes alone—not counting those put to death in concentration camps—was 77,000.[5]

These numbers are an indication of the potential for popular resistance in German society, and they reveal what happened to these potential resisters.

The intellectual source of the resistance against National Socialism manifested itself as soon as Hitler began his dictatorship. The theologian Dietrich Bonhoeffer, in an article in the Prussian conservative paper *Kreuz-Zeitung* on 26 February 1933, stated that Hitler's legitimacy depended on the Führer's acceptance of the superior divine authority.[6] The leader of the Social-Democratic Reichstag faction, Otto Wels, opposed the enabling bill in the Reichstag on 23 March 1933 and said: "We German Social Democrats declare in this historic hour solemnly our commitment to the principles of humanity and justice, liberty and socialism. No enabling act will give you the power to destroy ideas that are eternal and indestructible."[7] When Peter Yorck stood before the Nazi judge Roland Freisler on 7 August

1944, among the first group of conspirators to be tried for the 20 July 1944 coup, he gave the same reasons for his fundamental opposition to National Socialism: "The vital point in all this is the totalitarian claim of the state over the citizen to the exclusion of his religious and moral obligation to God."[8] Yorck was hanged on 8 August 1944.

The anti-Jewish measures motivated a good deal of popular resistance. Every time the authorities intensified the persecution, the level of criticism and of individual resistance also rose.[9] A great many of Hitler's underground opponents were motivated by the persecution of the Jews "above all," as the Gestapo noted in 1944.[10] After the 1938 pogrom Johannes Popitz, the Prussian minister of finance, went to see Göring to demand the punishment of those responsible for it and to tender his own resignation in protest against the outrages. But Göring only laughed and remarked that Popitz could hardly demand that the Führer be punished.[11] Popitz was persuaded to retain his post, only to use it for his own active part in the underground resistance. He was hanged on 2 February 1945.

Sociologically, all categories and classes of the population participated in the resistance, although the number of resisters was small. They included ordinary soldiers, professionals, factory workers, trade union leaders, diplomats, civil servants, generals, Catholic priests, and Lutheran ministers, and they represented the entire political spectrum from left to right. Broad support was lacking, however, nor could it be generated in the existing conditions, without a free press and under a police regime that criminalized and brutally punished the slightest utterance of criticism. Concentration camp thugs, compliant judges, the guillotine, and the hangman terrorized nearly everyone into submission, and nationalism did the rest to ensure loyalty to the regime in the war.

A few resistance groups managed to stay intact through the 1930s, some even longer. Communist, socialist, and Jewish resistance cells operated through the war.[12] Most churches resisted incorporation, although they collaborated with state authorities in nontheological matters.

A small number of churchmen, Bonhoeffer among them, wanted the churches to intervene if the government abused its powers. Bonhoeffer said in April 1933, in response to the government-ordered national "boycott" against Jewish businesses: "if the Church sees the state failing in its function of creating law and order, that is, if it sees the state producing without restraint too much or too little order and law," then the Church must "not merely dress the wounds of those who come under the wheel but must get hold of the wheel itself."[13]

In the spring of 1933, many priests and ministers rejected the National Socialists' leader cult and proclaimed openly from their pulpits that Christians had only one Führer, Jesus Christ. They openly equated the secular Führer with the Prince of the World, Satan. Then the massacre of SA leaders in 1934, and later the horrors of the concentration camps, intimidated church leaders as well as others. Hundreds of priests and ministers were sent to concentration camps; most of the others retreated to the position that they must attend to their parishioners' souls and merely comfort them when they suffered persecution and injustice. They generally used the words of the Gospels in ways that did not offend the authorities. In the face of the Pogrom of 1938, which many people referred to, with bitter irony, as "Reichskristallnacht," almost all priests and ministers were silent. Those few ministers and priests who spoke out were immediately imprisoned.

A few, like Bonhoeffer, decided that they must take direct political action, even without the support of their own Church.[14] But they could do it only underground. When Bonhoeffer was called up to military service, he obtained a sinecure in the military counterintelligence branch (OKW/Amt Ausland/Abwehr), where he worked to overthrow Hitler's government by traveling to Sweden and Switzerland to try to establish contacts abroad and to find Allied support for the German underground.

Using his position in the military intelligence service, he also helped Jews to escape deportation to the death camps. Three weeks before his arrest in April 1943 (for his part in a rescue operation for Jews), Bonhoeffer helped a committee of the Old Prussian Confessing Church synod's Council of Brethren prepare a statement on the Fifth Commandment. The committee included Peter Yorck, one of the chief conspirators against Hitler. The committee's work resulted in "Notes for Pastors and Elders on the Treatment of the Fifth Commandment." These "Notes" instructed all pastors to read from the pulpit on the annual day of repentance (mid-November) these words: "Woe to us and our nation if it is held to be justified to kill men because they are regarded as unworthy to live, or because they belong to another race."[15] Bonhoeffer was hanged on 9 April 1945.

There was a good deal more opposition here and there. The bishop of Münster, Clemens August von Galen, publicly condemned the mass murder of the feeble-minded and the mentally ill (but did not mention the murder of the Jews). Workers' groups sabotaged production in some factories, and some kept up contacts with Communist leaders in Moscow. But this sort of opposition, and whatever "popular" opposition was offered, was little more than an irritant to the regime. No dictatorial regime in recent history has been overthrown from within so long as it has commanded the loyalty of its armed forces. Effective opposition seemed possible, therefore, only from within the establishment and in conjunction with substantial elements of the armed forces. There were indeed two occasions when some of the highest-ranking military leaders offered direct opposition against Hitler's war plans.

The first occurred in November 1937 when Hitler announced some plans for his conquests to the heads of the armed forces. He had in mind, for now, Czechoslovakia and Austria, and, in the near future, a war against the western powers; after that he would look eastward for the greater spaces he said Germany needed. When he had spoken, there were objections—

from the war minister (Field Marshal von Blomberg), from the commander in chief of the army (General von Fritsch), from the foreign minister (Baron von Neurath), and from the commander in chief of the air force and designated successor to the Führer (General Göring). Thus, the Chancellor and Führer of Germany did not receive any support for his plans at this highest level of society, but by February 1938 the three principal objectors—Blomberg, Fritsch, and Neurath—had lost their posts.

The second occasion came when Hitler ordered a military attack against Czechoslovakia in 1938. The chief of the general staff of the army, Gen. Ludwig Beck remonstrated against Hitler's war plans with memoranda, and finally, in July and August 1938, he attempted to lead senior army commanders in a coup d'état against Hitler. Beck wanted them to confront Hitler during a conference in August 1938 and to put him on notice that they would not carry out an order to attack Czechoslovakia. Beck expected clashes with the SS and Hitler's arrest, but the plan failed because the commander in chief of the army, General von Brauchitsch, whom Hitler had bribed with financial aid for a divorce, denied Beck his support. Beck had no choice but to resign.

As the threat of war became obvious to all, the response of society at large paralleled that of these military and political leaders. When parts of the Second Mechanized Division from Stettin marched through the streets of Berlin on 27 September 1938, the Berliners flatly refused to cheer. The American news correspondent, William Shirer, noted that the "hundreds of thousands of Berliners pouring out of their offices . . . ducked into the subways, refused to look on, and the handful that did stood at the curb in utter silence. . . . It has been the most striking demonstration against the war that I've ever seen. . . . They are dead set against war."[16]

Hitler was furious. On 10 November 1938 in Munich, on the day after Kristallnacht, the nationwide pogrom that he had authorized, and with the synagogues still burning, he addressed four hundred journalists and publishers to say that circumstances had forced him to speak almost only of peace for decades, and that he believed that "that pacifist gramophone record" had played itself out. The entire people now must be indoctrinated to begin slowly to scream for violence, the government's true intentions could no longer be camouflaged, the truth had to be brutally stated.[17]

When Hitler maneuvered Germany into war a year later for what was presented to the nation as just grievances, when he won military campaigns against Poland and France in 1940 and launched one against the Soviet Union in 1941, it seemed impossible to overthrow him. At the same time the regime's crimes multiplied and increased immeasurably to include the methodical murder of millions of Jews, Poles, Russians, Sinti and Romanies (Gypsies), and Communists. These crimes produced more opposition. The bishop of Münster, Count von Galen, openly preached against "euthanasia" killings; the bishop of Württemberg, D. Theophil Wurm, sent his protests against the murder of the Jews directly to government ministers and to Hitler himself.

In 1942 and early in 1943, several students and a philosophy professor in the University of Munich secretly produced and distributed some seven thousand leaflets described as "Leaflets of the White Rose." The group posted the leaflets from mailboxes in Munich, Stuttgart, Augsburg, Frankfurt, Linz, and Vienna, to addresses chosen at random according to professions indicated in telephone directories.[18] The first leaflet called for resistance against the fraud of the so-called National Socialist world-view, against "the atheist war machine," against the unspeakable crimes of Hitler, against a state that claimed to be above justice and humanity. The second leaflet treated the murder of the Jews as "the most fearful crime against the dignity of man, a crime without parallel in the entire history of mankind" and as the central ethical issue of resistance. This leaflet noted that three hundred thousand Jews had been murdered in Poland since 1939, asking why the German people were apathetic in face of these crimes and how they could have become so brutalized and indifferent, and it accused them of co-responsibility. It called upon the German people to rise up in resistance. At a time, in February 1943, when the regime was nervous and insecure in the wake of the military catastrophe of the battle of Stalingrad, the White Rose group publicly distributed the leaflets in the University of Munich, hoping to start an insurrection. This led to their arrests and to the execution of the principals in February and July 1943.

As underground antigovernment activities failed, opposition at the highest level never again materialized as it had in 1937 and 1938. There were protests from high-ranking field commanders against mass murders by the SS, but none of the army and army-group commanders resigned his position on this issue; each was convinced that he could not "desert" his troops, who were engaged in mortal combat against the enemy.

Peter Count Yorck, a lawyer and civil servant, was a cousin of Claus Count Stauffenberg, who in July 1944 attempted to kill Hitler, and a friend of Helmuth James Count Moltke. In 1934 Yorck had begun to look for others who were opposed to the regime. He joined with Moltke in a group of resisters who foresaw the war and the collapse of Hitler's rule through the victory of the Allied powers. They had little or no confidence in the prospects of a military coup, and they pursued what might be described as a pacifist option of resistance. They actively helped to modify policies concerning hostages and helped Jews to escape; Moltke especially worked to keep German military practices in conformity with international law. But they did not actively support efforts to overthrow Hitler from within Germany until the autumn of 1943. They wanted to have plans ready for social and political reconstruction after the collapse, and they wanted to be ready for public service themselves. The group included socialists and trade-union leaders, economists, civil servants, professionals, and clergy. They held major meetings in

July 1941, May and October 1942, and June 1943. Some of the larger meetings took place at Moltke's estate of Kreisau in Silesia, but the friends met mainly in Berlin. Yorck's apartment at number 50 Hortensienstrasse became a center of anti-Hitler activity. The conspirators prepared plans for a reorganised, democratic German society, based on the concept of "small groups," self-government through locally elected bodies, and a tiered system of delegation up to the national government level. This was to ensure a true representation of the various social concerns and to avoid distortions caused by the self-interests of political parties. Yorck had a major part in the drafting of the group's constitutional plans. Most of Yorck's documents and letters were destroyed, but his central importance in the Kreisau group's activities emerges from the numerous references to Yorck in Moltke's letters, which did survive.[19] On 19 January 1944 Moltke was arrested because he had warned someone who was himself in danger of being arrested.[20] Seven members of the Kreisau group, including Yorck and Moltke, were hanged for their participation in the 20 July 1944 uprising.

Moltke believed, and Yorck shared this view, that it would be futile for opponents of National Socialism who would be needed for postwar reconstruction to sacrifice their lives in a hopeless conspiracy, and they believed that the defeat of Germany must be total in order to prevent the revival of a politically pernicious stab-in-the-back legend (after Germany's collapse in 1918 the extreme Right claimed that the revolutionaries of the Left had "stabbed" the fighting troops in the back, and it was widely believed that this agitation had helped Hitler in his rise to power).

But in the autumn of 1943, Col. Claus Stauffenberg joined the conspiracy. Peter Yorck and Claus Stauffenberg were cousins, and Moltke knew Claus's elder brother, Berthold, from his own work on government committees on international law in the 1930s. Claus Stauffenberg appeared to have the will and the ability to lead the conspiracy with a good chance of success.

Moltke now gave up his opposition to direct action. From August 1943 both Yorck and Moltke actively supported Stauffenberg's efforts to overthrow Hitler. From the early days of September 1943, Yorck, Moltke, and their friends Theodor Steltzer and Adam von Trott conferred with Berthold Stauffenberg about the uprising. Yorck arranged for Claus Stauffenberg to meet with the Social Democrat Julius Leber.[21]

Stauffenberg had become aware quite early, in 1939 when he was a captain, of what seemed to be isolated massacres in Poland, whose perpetrators had been prosecuted.[22] In the summer of 1941, now a major in the Army High Command Organization Branch, Stauffenberg asked a second lieutenant (Reserves) in the quartermaster section of the general staff, the historian Walther Bussmann, to collect all information that implicated the SS in crimes. Bussmann also informed Stauffenberg of reports that SS and police mobile killing squads were carrying out mass executions behind the German lines against alleged guerilla fighters, and Stauffenberg saw reports of deaths that ran into millions.[23]

Some resisters, like Stauffenberg or Moltke, who were searching for such information, became convinced rather late that indeed a systematic program of killing the Jews was in progress. Ulrich von Hassell and Carl Goerdeler had recorded their outrage at the mass murder of the Jews earlier.[24] The SS, of course, made great efforts to keep their operations secret. But the main obstacle to believing what was happening must have been its sheer unbelievability. It was apparently only in April and May 1942 that Stauffenberg became fully informed and convinced of what was happening: that the German police, the SS, and even some army forces were engaged in killing all Jews. Then and there Stauffenberg declared that Hitler must be killed.[25] Moltke took even longer to accept the systematic killings in concentration camps as fact, although he had been informed of it in March 1942 by his brother-in-law Hans Deichmann, who had traveled in the immediate vicinity of Auschwitz.

Only in October 1942 Moltke indicated in a letter to his wife that it all had to be accepted as fact.[26]

The murder of the Jews as a motivating force of the resistance against Hitler is commonly underestimated by historians, although it was not underestimated by the Gestapo, who summed up: "The entire alienation of the men of the reactionary conspiracy vis-à-vis the ideas of National Socialism finds expression most of all in their position on the Jewish Question. . . . they stubbornly maintain the liberal position of granting to the Jews fundamentally the same rights as to every other German."[27]

During 1942 and in January 1943, Stauffenberg sought to persuade senior commanders on the eastern front to lead a coup against Hitler, but to no avail. In February 1943 he was posted as senior staff officer to the Tenth Panzer Division in Tunisia, where in April he was badly wounded, and he recovered in a Munich military hospital until August. Now he was posted to a high staff position in Home Army Command in Berlin.

The military conspirators meanwhile, particularly in February and March 1943, plotted and attempted assassination attacks against Hitler, always in cooperation with the civilian wing of the anti-Hitler conspiracy, which was led by Goerdeler, Beck, and Hassell.[28]

From August 1943, after Stauffenberg's recovery, Stauffenberg and Brig. Henning von Tresckow led the planning. Stauffenberg had joined the civilian conspiracy reluctantly because he believed that only one established authority in society, the army, should remove the government.

Stauffenberg and Tresckow planned the seizure of power by Home Army forces. Their plans reveal the conspirators' assessment of the state of mind of German society: the Home Army was to be mobilized on the basis of a prevarication, namely, that corrupt elements within the Nazi Party and the SS had assassinated the Führer in order to put themselves into power, and that in this situation the army had assumed executive authority to protect the regime. The plotters had to try to manipulate a society that was presumably ready to repudiate crimes, death, and destruction, while at the same time it was, through nationalism, bound in loyal support to the chief criminal. But the true purpose of the conspiracy was revealed in the first general orders to the army and in proclamations to be broadcast by radio. They stressed the repudiation of all that the previous regime had done.

In June 1944 Stauffenberg himself gained the opportunity to attend some of Hitler's briefings. It was now clear that the assassination, the key to everything else, would not be carried out at all unless Stauffenberg himself, who had lost an eye, his right hand, and two fingers of his left hand, effected the assassination in Hitler's headquarters and acted as the leader of the coup in Berlin. The odds against his succeeding were staggering.[29]

The Home Army command and the government were in Berlin, Hitler's headquarters were near Salzburg in Austria, alternatively near Rastenburg in East Prussia—in either case about three hundred and fifty miles from Berlin.

Stauffenberg and his fellow plotters expected the uprising to begin in Berlin while Stauffenberg was at Hitler's headquarters. Even if Stauffenberg himself were killed, or for other reasons failed to return to Berlin, the uprising had to go forward in his absence.

But three generals among the conspirators insisted that Stauffenberg must kill Hitler only if he could at the same time kill Göring, Hitler's official successor, and Himmler, the powerful leader of the SS. Göring and Himmler were dangerous, but it was unrealistic to wait for a time when Stauffenberg could catch them together with Hitler. One opportunity to assassinate Hitler was therefore wasted, on 11 July 1944. When the next opportunity came for Stauffenberg to attend Hitler's briefing, on 15 July 1944, the generals in the plot had not told Stauffenberg that they still insisted that he could kill Hitler only if he could kill Göring and Himmler at the same time. Stauffenberg flew to Hitler's headquarters early in the morning, just before 8 A.M.

His associate in Berlin, Col. Albrecht Mertz von Quirnheim, ordered the mobilization of the troops around Berlin that were to occupy the capital. But after Stauffenberg's arrival at Hitler's headquarters, one of the generals in the plot informed him that he must not activate his "bomb" unless Göring and Himmler were there.

Stauffenberg and Mertz saw that they had been deserted by their co-conspirators, whose support was crucial for the success of the coup. Nevertheless, they decided to act without the generals' consent. Stauffenberg was not prepared to go on indefinitely carrying "bombs" into Hitler's headquarters and was determined to carry out the assassination whether Göring and Himmler were present or not. But when Stauffenberg tried to proceed with the assassination attack, he was physically prevented by one of the conspiring generals from placing his "bomb" in Hitler's briefing.

On 20 July 1944 he disregarded the older conspirators' reservations completely. He had no illusions that his action would be supported in Berlin or elsewhere. Preparatory mobilizations as on 15 July could not be repeated.

While setting his fuse, just before Hitler's midday situation briefing, Stauffenberg was interrupted by an orderly. This unsettled him so that he went off with half of the explosives he had brought with him. The "bomb" was designed to kill all those present at Hitler's situation briefing, but with only half the power, the device killed only one person immediately, three died later, and Hitler escaped with bruises.

There was no reasonable hope that an assassin could leave the security zones of the headquarters after an assassination attack, or even after any explosion. Against all odds, Stauffenberg bluffed his way through and, three hours later, reached Berlin to take command of the coup. He found there in the command center, among others, Peter Yorck ready to help and to share the fate of his fellow conspirators.

But the coup d'état never gained momentum, mainly because

of the three-hour delay and the news that Hitler had survived. The declared basis for the army taking over executive power manifestly did not exist. Late that evening Stauffenberg and three of his comrades were shot in the Home Army Command courtyard, General Beck took his own life, and close to two hundred other resisters, with Yorck among the first eight of them, were subsequently hanged. Claus Stauffenberg's brother Berthold was hanged, resuscitated, and hanged again several times, and the hangings were filmed for Hitler.

Stauffenberg and his friends, like the students of the White Rose, knew that there was almost no chance of success. They acted in the face of overwhelming odds, without substantial hope of either killing Hitler or seizing control in Germany. They had even less hope of surviving politically for more than a few days or weeks after a *successful* coup and no hope of putting into effect their reconstruction concepts. In the face of Allied war aims, they had no hope of avoiding the occupation, amputation, and division of Germany by enemy forces. But they all agreed: the assassination had to be attempted at all costs, and even if that failed, the attempt to seize power in Berlin had to be made. What mattered was no longer the practical purpose of the coup, but the proof to the world that men and women of the resistance had dared to take the decisive step and were giving their lives to uphold their beliefs.[30] This was what many had done who came from all walks of life, and from all over the social and political spectrum.

Marion Yorck's story and a cursory review of some of the names of the leading conspirators involved in the 20 July 1944 uprising may suggest a prominence of "the nobility." It is true that many members of the nobility served in the armed forces, as a matter of tradition. It is also true that many noblemen believed that it was not only their duty but their privilege to fight and to die for their fatherland.[31] But generally, officers of the nobility were far from a majority in the officer corps. The social structure of the officer corps had been changing in Prussia and in other German states since the beginning of the nineteenth century, when the criteria for admission to officer candidacy had been widened to include men of the middle classes. Of all German officers of general or admiral rank between 1933 and 1945 who were born between 1881 and 1900, only 18 percent came from families of the nobility.[32]

An examination of the identities of the resisters shows that of the approximately seven hundred who were arrested and of the approximately two hundred who were hanged for their part in the uprising, the majority were neither nobles nor military officers.

Additionally, a vastly larger number of the nobility served loyally in the armed forces and in other positions during the National Socialist dictatorship than the number who engaged in resistance to it. As in every social stratum or category, so in the nobility the resisters were a minority. The majority served their government loyally throughout; a small number in fact became infamous as perpetrators of war crimes and crimes against humanity.

Any closer examination of the background of the resisters will indicate that character and the conviction that every person had a responsibility to try to avert evil and to prevent further crimes were more important criteria for turning a person into a resister than social origin or status.

Two days before his execution, Peter Yorck wrote in a letter concerning his part in the attempted uprising that he had been driven to it "by the feeling of guilt that weighs on all of us."[33] Yorck, his cousin Stauffenberg, and many others, were deeply afflicted by the number and enormity of crimes committed in the German name. Under Gestapo interrogation Yorck singled out for his condemnation the "extermination measures" against Jews, and in the "People's Court" trial in which he was condemned to death by hanging, he confirmed his own and his cousin Stauffenberg's loathing at the persecution of the Jews, which the presiding judge, Roland Freisler, referred to as "the extermination of the Jews."[34] Axel von dem Bussche, referring to the mass shooting of Jews he had witnessed at Dubno on 5 October 1942, declared that "the twentieth of July in essence would not have happened without those things."[35] Claus Stauffenberg had said to a fellow-officer in 1943, "As General Staff officers we are all co-responsible."[36] The guilt that Yorck and Stauffenberg accepted was that they had been too slow to oppose the evil and that they had been inactive in helpless outrage too long after they had seen it.[37]

Their self-sacrificial attempts to resist Hitler cannot serve as an alibi for other Germans, but they gave Germany a moral perspective for facing her recent history.

PETER HOFFMANN

Notes

1. Ian Kershaw, *Hitler, 1889–1936: Hubris* (New York: W. W. Norton, 1999), 370. The often repeated sweeping generalization that the German republic lacked the support of its voters is a half-truth. In 1932, 64 percent of the electorate (of whom the approximately 17 percent Communist voters did not support democracy, and of whom the 8.9 percent German National People's Party supporters' democratic position was questionable) did not vote for the National Socialists.

2. See Henry Ashby Turner Jr., *Hitler's Thirty Days to Power: January 1933* (Reading MA: Addison-Wesley, 1996).

3. See *Documents on British Foreign Policy 1919–1939*, 2nd ser., vol. 6 (London: H. M. Stationery Office, 1957), 381–85, 649–53.

4. Franz W. Seidler, *Die Militärgerichtsbarkeit der Deutschen Wehrmacht 1939–1945: Rechtsprechung und Strafvollzug* (Munich: Herbig, 1991), 44 states that 10,191 death sentences against soldiers and employees of the armed forces were handed down until and including November 1944; he bases this upon Rolf-Dieter Breitenstein and Philipp Joachim, "Die imperialistische Militärgerichtsbarkeit von 1898 bis 1945" (Jur. Diss., Humboldt-Universität, Berlin, 1983), 233, and a file in Militärarchiv Potsdam W-10-1168.

5. *Trial of the Major War Criminals before the International Military Tribunal, Nuremberg, 14 November 1945–1 October 1946* vol. 38 (Nuremberg: Secretariat of the Tribunal, 1949), 362–65; Martin Broszat, "Nationalsozialistische Konzentrationslager 1933 bis 1945," in *Konzentrationslager, Kommissarbefehl, Judenverfolgung*, ed. Martin Broszat, Hans-Adolf Jacobsen, Helmut Krausnick (Olten-Freiburg im Breisgau: Walter-Verlag, 1965), 158–59; Eric H. Boehm, ed., *We Survived: The Stories of Fourteen of the Hidden and the Hunted of Nazi Germany* (New Haven CT: Yale University Press, 1949), viii, based on records of the Secret State Police; Gabriel A. Almond, "The German Resistance Movement," *Current History* 10 (1946), 409–527; Wolfgang Sofsky, *Die Ordnung des Terrors: Das Konzentrationslager* (Frankfurt am Main: S. Fischer, 1993), 56–57; further Walter Wagner, *Der Volksgerichtshof im nationalsozialistischen Staat* (Stuttgart: Deutsche Verlags-Anstalt, 1974), 945; Manfred Messerschmidt, Fritz Wüllner, *Die Wehrmachtjustiz im Dienste des Nationalsozialismus. Zerstörung einer Legende* (Baden-Baden: Nomos Verlag, 1987), 49–50, 70, 73.

6. Dietrich Bonhoeffer, "Drei Führertypen in der jungen Generation," *Kreuz-Zeitung*, 26 Feb. 1933.

7. *Verhandlungen des Reichstags VIII, Wahlperiode 1933*, vol. 457 (Berlin: Reichsdruckerei, 1934), 34.

8. *Trial* vol. 33, 424.

9. Sarah Gordon, *Hitler, Germans and the "Jewish Question"* (Princeton: Princeton University Press, 1984).

10. *Spiegelbild einer Verschwörung: Die Kaltenbrunner-Berichte an Bormann und Hitler über das Attentat vom 20. Juli 1944. Geheime Dokumente aus dem ehemaligen Reichssicherheitshauptamt* (Stuttgart: Seewald Verlag, 1961), 449–50, 457, 471.

11. Ulrich von Hassell, *Die Hassell-Tagebücher 1938–1944: Aufzeichnungen vom Andern Deutschland* (Berlin: Siedler Verlag, 1988), 70 (Engl. edn abridged).

12. Cf. Arnold Paucker, *Jewish Resistance in Germany: The Facts and the Problems* (Berlin: Gedenkstätte Deutscher Widerstand, 1991).

13. Dietrich Bonhoeffer, *Gesammelte Schriften*, vol. 2 (Munich: Chr. Kaiser Verlag, 1959), 45, 48–49.

14. Bonhoeffer to Reinhold Niebuhr June 1939 in Bonhoeffer, *Gesammelte Schriften*, vol. 1, 3rd ed. (1978), 320; Eberhard Bethge, "Dietrich Bonhoeffer und die Juden," in Ernst Feil and Ilse Tödt, eds., *Konsequenzen: Dietrich Bonhoeffers Kirchenverständnis heute*, (Munich: Chr. Kaiser Verlag, 1980), 198–201.

15. Eberhard Bethge, *Dietrich Bonhoeffer: Theologian, Christian, Contemporary* (London: Collins, 1970), 613.

16. William L. Shirer, *Berlin Diary: The Journal of a Foreign Correspondent, 1934–1941* (New York: Alfred A. Knopf 1941), 142–43.

17. Wilhelm Treue, ed., "Rede Hitlers vor der deutschen Presse (10. November 1938)," *Vierteljahrshefte für Zeitgeschichte* 6 (1958), 175–91.

18. The White Rose, *The Resistance by Students against Hitler: Munich 1942/43* (Munich: The White Rose Foundation, 1991).

19. Helmuth James von Moltke, *Letters to Freya: 1939–1945*, ed. and trans. Beate Ruhm von Oppen (New York: Alfred A. Knopf, 1990), passim.

20. The following are generally the basis for the text that follows and provide an overview of the subject: Ger van Roon, *Neuordnung im Widerstand. Der Kreisauer Kreis innerhalb der deutschen Widerstandsbewegung* (Munich: R. Oldenbourg, 1967); abridged in English as *German Resistance to Hitler: Count von Moltke and the Kreisau Circle*, trans. Peter Ludlow (London: Van Nostrand Reinhold, 1971); Michael Balfour and Julian Frisby, *Helmuth von Moltke: A Leader against Hitler* (London: Macmillan, 1972).

21. Peter Hoffmann, *Stauffenberg: A Family History, 1905–1944* (Cambridge: Cambridge University Press, 1995), 187, 190, 193, 194.

22. Hoffmann, *Stauffenberg*, 113, 115–16.

23. Hoffmann, *Stauffenberg*, 133.

24. Peter Hoffmann, "The Persecution of the Jews as a Motive for Resistance Against National Socialism," in *The Moral Imperative: New Essays on the Ethics of Resistance in National Socialist Germany, 1933–1945*, ed. Andrew Chandler (Boulder CO: Westview Press, 1998), 73–104; Peter Hoffmann, "The German Resistance, the Jews, and Daniel Goldhagen," in *Hyping the Holocaust. Scholars Answer Goldhagen*, ed.

Franklin H. Littell (East Rockaway NY: Cummings & Hathaway, 1997), 73–88.

25. Hoffmann, *Stauffenberg*, 145, 151.

26. Hans Deichmann, pocket diary 1942 and interview with the author 23 July 1989; Helmuth James von Moltke, *Briefe an Freya 1939–1945*, ed. Beate Ruhm von Oppen (Munich: Verlag C. H. Beck, 1988), 355–56, 420 (Engl. ed. slightly abridged). On the beginning of mass killings of Jews with gas in Auschwitz on 3 September 1941 and January 1942 in Birkenau see Eugen Kogon, Hermann Langbein, Adalbert Rückerl, ed., *Nationalsozialistische Massentötungen durch Giftgas: Eine Dokumentation*, 2nd ed., (Frankfurt am Main: S. Fischer Verlag, 1983), 194–206.

27. *Spiegelbild*, 471.

28. Peter Hoffmann, *German Resistance to Hitler* (Cambridge MA: Harvard University Press, 1988), 110–11; Peter Hoffmann, *The History of the German Resistance, 1933–1945*, 3rd ed. (Montreal: McGill-Queen's University Press, 1996), chapter 9.

29. For this and subsequent paragraphs see Hoffmann, *Stauffenberg*, 234–77.

30. Hoffmann, *Stauffenberg*, 238.

31. Rudolf-Christoph, Freiherr von Gersdorff, *Soldat im Untergang*, (Frankfurt am Main: Ullstein, 1977), 18.

32. Reinhard Stumpf, *Die Wehrmacht-Elite: Rang- und Herkunftsstruktur der deutschen Generale und Admirale 1933–1945* (Boppard am Rhein: Boldt, 1982), 235, 237, 280, 301.

33. Yorck to Marion von Yorck 6 August 1944; Marion von Yorck, letter to the author 10 Aug. 1972.

34. *Spiegelbild*, 110; *Trial* 33, 424.

35. Axel von dem Bussche, interview by author, 19 July 1984.

36. Nina Countess von Stauffenberg in Joachim Kramarz, *Stauffenberg: The Architect of the Famous July Twentieth Conspiracy to Assassinate Hitler*, trans. R. H. Barry (New York: Macmillan, 1967), 132.

37. Hoffmann, *Stauffenberg*, xiv.

The Power of Solitude

I

TODAY IT IS NOT AT ALL a matter of course that as an old person you still live in the city where you were born and where you have actually spent most of your life. I grew up here in Berlin in Grunewald and also went to school here. There were six of us children, four girls and two boys; I was the third. While we quarreled now and again, it never came to blows. But we also didn't treat each other delicately—in complete contrast to the Yorck siblings.

My mother, Else Winter, was a rather dour woman. She came from the Westphalian Springorum family and was twenty-three when I was born. Her mother was a Waldhausen from the Rhineland, but with my mother the Westphalian side predominated. With me it was perhaps the Rhenish side that prevailed. Although my mother was not exactly strict, she was very reserved toward strangers. However, she had a very good manner in dealing with our longtime household help. There was always peace, and she was loved very much; our household was her closed kingdom.

During the First World War, my father, Franz Winter, born in 1862, was a reserve officer with the Fourth Guard Fusilier Regiment, called the Maikäfer. He was drafted and sent to Niš in Serbia as a city commandant. He didn't go to the front—by then he was already too old for that.

Our dear nanny was very important. Her name was Schröder, but we called her Röder, and she really treated us as a mother would. Unlike today, at that time there was frequently a kind of intermediary between children and parents; mothers had no direct dealings with their children, at least not in the large families. So for many years Röder was actually like a mother to us, and sometimes there was a tense relationship between our two mothers.

When the First World War broke out we happened to be at Röder's mother's place in Güstrow. Two weeks later we went home. Father picked us up at the Stettin train station, and I still recall that I saw him and ran up to him screaming because I had imagined that he was dead. Because "war" at that time was to me the same as "being dead."

Later it was different because in the first year of the war, when nothing but victories were being celebrated, my grandmother always invited us for cake at the Hilbrich pastry shop. Then war simply meant "victory."

We children had very different relationships with our parents. I was really always more my father's daughter. When I was very small, he used to call his dogs around five o'clock in the afternoon and would walk through the Grunewald or Messel park. And for me it was the greatest pleasure to go with him, unless my mother went with him. Because he took such gigantic steps I hopped along side of him in three-quarter time. What we talked about I no longer remember, but just being with him was enough to make me happy.

During school vacations our parents naturally always traveled with us children, as was usual then. My father preferred to sit alone in a compartment. He would take, at the most, one or two of the children with him; the others sat in another compartment. And when the train stopped at a station, we had to go to Father and make wild faces at the window, so that no stranger would even think of sitting next to him.

On these vacations we usually traveled either to the mountains or to the ocean. Very often our Springorum grandparents came along. My grandfather was even more unapproachable than my mother. You felt honored if he so much as tapped your fingers. He was a mining civil official and also had a mine, and on his desk lay the most curious stones. Of course for us children those were the most beautiful things, and when we touched them, he flicked our fingers with a ruler. But I never held that against him.

I went to a school that was considered very progressive even then. It was the Grunewald Gymnasium, the present day Walther-Rathenau-Gymnasium, a so-called *Aufbauschule*, where from the tenth grade on one could choose to add subjects or do the usual ones in a more intensive fashion. I took intensive courses in Greek and Latin. Later that "recommended" me to my future husband.

There were only a few of us in the class at that time. Next to me sat Ursula Andreae, now von Mangoldt, and Dietrich Bonhoeffer also sat in the same row. I am still in touch only with Ulla Mangoldt. It was a mixed school, by the way, the only one of its kind in Berlin; and in the class were four girls and eight boys. We girls got no grade for citizenship because Principal Vilmar, as professor of Middle High German, thought that the girls had to behave themselves so well anyway that it was not worth mentioning!

Ulla was my best friend. She lived across from us. Usually I went over to her house in the afternoons, and we sat together and chatted. Sometimes she also came over to my house. She had, however, a certain shyness in front of my father, who was friendly toward her and that's about all. On the other hand, I was afraid of her mother, a sister of Walther Rathenau and a brilliant woman. At that time I perceived her as frightening with her quick-witted and cutting pronouncements. And when I knew that she was home, I went through the kitchen entrance to see Ulla, because that way I could visit her without being challenged.

Denominational matters really played no role in our circle of friends. As a matter of fact, half the students in our school in Grunewald were Jewish! In those days we didn't pay any attention to such differences. It was not until the beginning of the Third Reich that we took any notice of those differences, and I never accepted them.

Politics didn't interest me until the Third Reich, when I was at Peter's side. In the Weimar Republic I was still completely apolitical, and I recall only the horror that the class experienced when Ulla Mangoldt's uncle, Walther Rathenau, was murdered in 1922 very close to the school. That was like an intrusion into our idyllic world.

My upbringing was Christian, but without any church affiliation. I cannot recall that my parents ever went to church or were friends with pastors. And later Peter and I preferred to be in the forest, where we found God in nature; we didn't start going to church until 1943. Of course Ulla Mangoldt and Dietrich Bonhoeffer later studied theology; they most likely got the impetus to do that in our school.

We had a teacher by the name of Kappus who had originally been a tutor for the princes Louis Ferdinand and his brothers. He was said to have spoken eleven different languages. He was a charming man, very short, with a large head, and he also happened to speak Hebrew. Ulla and Dietrich and two others learned Hebrew from him, in order to be able to read the Old Testament in its original language. That was probably how they became interested in theology, at least Ulla.

Exactly how Dietrich Bonhoeffer became interested in it I don't know. His father, of course, was a famous psychiatrist, after whom the Bonhoeffer clinics are named. I often visited them, at least once a month for lunch. Dietrich also came to our house or to Ulla's; we were a nice clique.

At the outbreak of the First World War I was ten years old. This war and the defeat in 1918 turned the people's thinking inside out. All that had to do with Kaiser Wilhelm crumbled. My father, however, was and remained true to the Kaiser. When he heard about his abdication he cried—he was full of despair.

Nevertheless, as we grew up, our parents did not steer us into certain tracks, nor did they lead us by the hand. Of course we learned hard work, love of truth, decency, and, because there were six of us children, also mutual respect.

Incidentally, young people felt political change much more

strongly in art than in politics, which always progresses at a slower pace. I am thinking about Kortner's *Richard III*, produced by Jessner, and my father's horror over this performance. But we could not discuss it with him.

Perhaps it is the characteristic of an undemocratic time to accept politics as something given, something that cannot be influenced. Only art expressed something that moved us. In exactly the same way Peter and I later experienced theater and, above all, concerts in the Third Reich. And I remember Peter's profound joy when he heard the *Unfinished Symphony* or Beethoven's violin concerto. Art, especially music, gave him the feeling for beauty and freedom in a time that greatly troubled him.

During my school years I went twice to Sweden. I think it was for three months each time. During the first visit alone I gained seventeen pounds, because by the end of the First World War we ate almost nothing but potato bread, and we were all as skinny as wires. And yet we had a dear baker woman on the corner of Fasanenstrasse and Lietzenburgerstrasse, where we went once a week with a laundry basket because, after all, we had to get bread for ten people. Our baker woman always gave us something more for the ration cards because she liked us kids. However, I recall that the bread was so soggy that we often found potato peels still in it.

In Sweden I also fell in love for the first time, but it was an unhappy love. I think a first love should always be unhappy for a girl; whether that is also true for a boy I don't know. A girl learns so much in the process: in fact, she only becomes able to build a marriage when she doesn't go into it with full sails, deeply in love and ablaze.

Right from the beginning my relationship to Peter was, in any case, different from this first love affair, when I thought I had everything but the Grunewald Lake.

That was in 1919 or 1920, so I was fifteen or sixteen. I was again invited to Sweden, to Stockholm, by the local theater director, John Forsell, a friend of my father. This director made something reasonable out of the insecure, angular girl I was at that time. In the truest sense of the word he taught me how to walk. He noticed that I considered myself to be bad and exceptionally ugly, both inwardly and outwardly, and therefore as insecure as I could possibly be. He did not agree with that, and his opinion made me feel much more at ease. It also made me very happy to see how this Swedish family lived together. For example, they bathed together nude, and in such a natural way that was completely new to me and that would have been unimaginable in our family. Everything was totally natural and full of love. We were raised differently in this respect! We did not give free rein to our feelings. Nevertheless, I still think that our reserved upbringing did not hurt us. And besides myself, all of my siblings stuck to it. These rational principles that we received in our upbringing, these attitudes toward life, did give us stability. Although you sometimes had a different opinion, you didn't state your opposition loudly and definitely didn't ask as many questions as the children of today. My childhood was also far from the active and exciting one of my grandnephews and -nieces of today. We grew up more quietly, virtually encapsulated, without the stimuli of radio, television, or the possibility of individual, artistic, or athletic development.

I then finished school and later began to study at the university. It was medicine in the first semester, but anatomy, with which one had to begin, scared me off. In any case, I thought it was good to learn to think logically, which wasn't my strength. As a result I studied law. My father was very happy about that because he was always afraid that one of his daughters might end up in the theater. He was the general administrative director of all national (formerly royal) theaters and a very popular bureaucratic boss in the difficult terrain between government administration and artistic souls! At that time the Opera Unter den Linden and the Theater am Gendarmenmarkt, as well as the theaters in Kassel and Wiesbaden, belonged to the state theaters as a result of the War of 1866. Therefore, my father always had seats in the opera and theater. And so I could often go to the theater after my law classes with my university friends Oscar Schlitter and Klaus Curtius, whose father later became the Reich foreign minister.

I also still recall that my father was called every morning—even before breakfast—by the main cashier, who gave him the receipts of the previous evening. People were so Prussian and thrifty then that these daily receipts were precisely recorded. There simply were no subsidies like there are today.

We also had connections to Max Reinhardt through Ulla Mangoldt's mother, because she received tickets for the Reinhardt Theaters. So in the different Berlin theaters we saw at that time almost all the classics: Shakespeare's plays, the *Prinz von Homburg* produced by Jürgen Fehling, and *Orpheus in der Unterwelt* by Reinhardt. It was a fabulous evening when the whole public sang and laughed along, really quite a show.

There is not much more to tell about the university. I studied only in Berlin, and I know that we had excellent teachers. For example, Martin Wolff, a short man who barely reached the podium and whose seminars and lectures were so full that one usually had to stand. The coats were hanging on the windows, and the professor was speaking with a fine, soft voice, but you could have heard a pin drop, there was such an expectant hush.

There were, at that time, not only Germans attending the lecture, but even some blacks and many French-speaking students from Lebanon and North Africa.

Wolff was the author of a famous civil law text book. He was a Jew and, in the Third Reich, he had to leave immediately. He went to England, but thanks to his English wife that was not difficult for him. The class exercises with Wolff were very difficult. There were only twenty-two students in the seminars, and I was the only girl. I really had to pull myself together.

I also still remember Professors Kohlrausch and Goldschmidt, with whom I studied criminal law and civil procedure law; they made such an impression on the students because they spoke freely and in a lively fashion and did not read off a manuscript. I studied under Martin Wolff for several semesters and cannot remember that he ever repeated himself.

After six semesters I took my law exam, much to the joy of my father. He was extraordinarily proud of his daughter, whereas, to tell the truth, I was not so hot for law. I would probably not study it again today—more likely biology.

During my studies I also was not at all interested in politics. I didn't get into the habit of reading the newspaper until after the Second World War. At that time none of my friends read the *Völkischer Beobachter*. After the First World War we children were simply starved, starved for life as well! We read no newspapers. At that time I had not even thought about taking a stand or even keeping informed about politics. I was not a good citizen!

At home we felt the inflation after the First World War and the economic problems of the twenties only because money was gradually becoming scarce for our parents. They sold their beautiful house on Kronberger Street and moved to Zehlendorf. But that didn't bother us. We were just very thrifty, due perhaps to our Prussian upbringing. Every morning that I had classes at eight at the university, I got up at five or six, for the ride in the street car lasted at least an hour—I rarely took a taxi. Still today, when I get into one and it smells like cold smoke, I think of my father and have a guilty conscience. He said that taking a taxi indicated poor time management. He himself, however, had a car with a chauffeur by the name of August. I learned to drive with August when I was not yet of age, and once we were caught on the Avus. It was found out that I did not yet have a driver's license, and I got a ticket for over a hundred marks. I registered a protest and defended myself at the local court in Charlottenburg in front of the criminal judge. I said to the judge, "Do you know I have no income whatsoever, and why should parents have to pay for the mistakes of their children? And anyway, a hundred marks is a lot for a civil servant with six children." The fine was cut in half.

We four girls each had an allowance of twenty marks a month until we married, but I never thought, oh, that is not very much money. Ulla Mangoldt, by the way, thought the same. It may sound frivolous, but at that time we were very young and actually experienced only the beautiful aspects of the twenties: the wonderful theater, the dances and the grand balls. I especially remember one ball. It was at the Stresemann's, the foreign minister at that time. I had a wonderful dress of red taffeta, made from an old ball gown of my mother's that Mrs. Stresemann liked very much. Klaus Curtius, my fellow student, was also there. It must have been about 1928. Around midnight Mrs. Stresemann arranged a polonaise of the dancers leading to her husband's study. I can still see him sitting at his desk with very astonished eyes, a little startled at the boisterous youth intruding into the peacefulness of his work. A year later, in 1929, he died.

Politics, as I said, was rarely discussed. With the Reichstag election of 1930 Hitler became a threatening factor. My father was in fact very worried because he had a Jewish grandfather, so I had a Jewish great-grandfather. But I was simply full of life and *joie de vivre*. In 1933 my father once said to Peter and me, "You poor children, in what sort of times will you have to live!" But I thought, "Oh, I am living, and life is beautiful."

2

IN APRIL 1928 I went to my godfather Köckritz's daughter's wedding in Silesia, where I had never been before in my life. I canceled a trip to Sweden that I had wanted to take with my father and started on my way. The Köckritz estate was called Mondschütz. It was a lovely old castle surrounded by a moat, and I can still see myself sitting at a big table there in the evening: here the seat for the father of the bride, then me, and next to me an empty seat. They said someone else was expected, and he was coming on a motorcycle. The weather was bad, so we were waiting for him. A short time later he appeared, sat down in the empty seat next to me, and said to me in a way I found to be quite presumptuous, "I know your telephone number." I answered him, "You are not the only one."

That was my first meeting with Peter. I thought he was quite arrogant and derisive, at least that was what especially struck me then. I know, however, that from that day on he looked at no other girl. He later told me he was already wondering at that time whether I was possibly already engaged or perhaps a Catholic (I was neither). We danced the whole time and conversed wonderfully. The day after the wedding ceremony we walked for hours around the castle along the moat and talked about literature and religion.

I then went home with another date. All the same, Peter and I had arranged a meeting here at the train station in Halensee on the following Saturday; that was at the beginning of May. When I arrived home the first thing I did was to sit down and write a letter to cancel our date. I wrote: "It is better if we don't see each other again. You occupy me in such a way that I don't know where it might lead." I had the feeling I would lose myself and my independence and even the opening into life. I was simply afraid. On this same Saturday the phone rang at two thirty. My father answered and said only: "It's for you." He never asked who it was when someone called for us children, for he trusted us a great deal. Apparently Peter was already quite near our house. We then met immediately at the Roseneck. We went into the Grunewald; we lay down in the sun, and during the entire walk I never found out whether he had gotten my letter or not, so skillfully did he talk around it. Then I brought him home, and he and my father soon understood each other very well. Less so with my mother. He did not have the talent to be immediately so uninhibited and at ease; he came off at first as very taciturn, almost reserved, although he was polite. My mother could not quite warm up to him. The two of them were never able to do that.

Then we went together for two years. Peter was at that time in practical training in Silesia, in Oppeln, and when he wasn't in Berlin he wrote me every day. These early letters were burned, as were almost all of the later ones. I had entrusted them to a children's nurse in Kleinöls because after the Twentieth of July I feared that there would be house searches, and I wanted to go to Berlin. But when the Gestapo came and searched the manor, the woman, out of fear of placing her parents under suspicion, burned all the letters. When I later got out of jail and wanted to get them, Peter died a second time with his letters.

At that time he came very often on his motorcycle to Berlin, perhaps every other weekend. We walked together a lot in the Grunewald and went to the theater in the evenings. He stayed here with his sister Püzze Siemens; and almost every evening we had long telephone conversations, which his sister called "telephone devotions," although she never even found out with whom he was talking!

Finally he proposed to me. He asked me whether I wanted us to "hang up our clotheslines together," and I said, "Yes."

My father, who was almost twenty years older than my mother, was worried that my relationship with Peter, who was with us frequently during this time, was becoming too strong. He considered him too young for me and thought that when Peter was forty, I would already be an older woman and he only in his prime. But he put no obstacles in the way of our marriage. (In 1934 my father shot himself because he was very sick. That was terrible for me, for I loved him very much. He had a self-possessed, strong personality, and many people courted him, so to speak. Furthermore, I know that even my husband's oldest sister, Püzze Siemens, was totally enthralled with him, while on the other hand, she was at first not so happy that I took her brother away from her!)

In 1928 I went for the first time to Kleinöls, the manor of the Yorck family in Silesia, for a partridge hunt. For me it was like heaven. In September the sun shines there in a way that you just can't imagine, and the dogs sweat and roll themselves in the wet sand and look as though they came directly out of the wild. Besides that, the expanse of the landscape, the fertile fields, where beets and potatoes were not yet harvested, the cane forest, and pervading all of it this sun. . . . The people seemed more open and warm to me than elsewhere; I immediately formed good, completely natural relationships. The Yorck family was loved here, and I soon became "Countess Peter."

Peter then introduced me to the man who would later become my thesis supervisor, the specialist in state law, privy councillor Hans Helfritz. My topic was "Does the Tariff Contract Belong to Public Law?" How I decided the question, I no longer know. In any case Peter and I went to work on it together. At that time Peter lived here in Berlin on Duisburger Strasse. He completed his last phase as a law clerk in the Superior Court of Justice before his licensing exam. We drafted the outline together and wrote, I thought, a very nice doctoral thesis. When I showed it to Helfritz in the winter of 1928–29 he said only, "It seems like a bouquet of flowers to me!" For of course Peter had a different style. However, it all went smoothly, and on 28 June 1929 I became a Doctor of Law.

For a woman to get a doctorate was rather unusual then. Actually it was my father who had wanted it so much; he was proud of me and always encouraged me. And besides, by then I really liked law. Later on I became much more interested in criminal law than in civil law—it deals more with human destinies.

However, the idea of working at some point did not occur to me then. I wanted to have children. I was not quite finished with my practical training when I married. It's true that shortly after the wedding I had completed three years and could have registered for the exam, but I was somewhat fearful. I still think today that marriage is very stressful for a young girl, and it is a tremendous adjustment, a deep cut into her physical and emotional life! Today a young woman would probably decide differently.

So on 29 June 1929, we celebrated at Kleinöls. Peter's mother knew by then that we would get married. She had prepared a beautiful room for me, and Peter's brothers were quite curious to know for whom she had done it and why. Along with my doctorate we also celebrated the birthday of Peter's mother. Someone had woven a laurel wreath, and my older brother-in-law Paul, called Bia, gave a speech in Latin. Almost all the siblings were there. We sat at a big table in the garden room, and everyone was happy. Suddenly Peter's mother took the laurel wreath from my head, put a rose wreath in its place, and said, "Now comes something much more important than the doctorate, today we celebrate Marion as Peter's fiancée." And then she gave a charming speech.

I really got along wonderfully with her. She was an incredibly loving person. She had hair like finely spun silk, was very sensitive, and lived with her whole heart exclusively for the family. She was also the center of the family, and the children loved her immensely. In everything they did she was foremost in their minds; if one traveled to Berlin, one had to call immediately to say that one had arrived safely and so on. This family devoured me, so to speak; my own siblings from that point on got the short end of the stick. Also my parents. In the Bible it says the husband should be devoted to his wife, but for me it was the other way around. I got along with Peter's siblings better than with my own. At home it seemed to me that—how should I say—something in intellectual richness was missing, while with these Kleinölser children each was really a personality in his own right. There were four brothers and six sisters: Paul (called Bia), Peter, Hans (called Hannusch), and the youngest, Heinrich. And there were the sisters Bertha (called Püzze), Davida (called Dävy), Nina, Dorothea, Renate, and the youngest, Irene. Davida married into the Moltke family, Nina into the Prittwitz family, Bertha into the Siemens family, and Renate into the Gersdorff family. The youngest sister, called Muto, was born in 1913, and when I met her in 1928 at Kleinöls she was already an affectionate, loving, fifteen-year-old girl. With her I always felt quite close and intimate. We loved each other. I also supported her so that she was allowed to study at the university. Peter's mother did not think that was right at first. And her spiteful brothers said to her, "You may become a nurse, but that is the most that you will achieve." And yet she became a very good doctor. She could speak with people and divine, so to speak, the emotional or physical state in which they found themselves. Muto was an astonishing person. To be sure, it was difficult for her when she became gravely ill after the war; but even then she had this floating, light quality that was so characteristic of her and at the same time an intensity. After the war I went with her five times across the Neisse illegally; we were in jail together in 1945, in Breslau, Schweidnitz, and finally in Warsaw—all that was perhaps too much for her delicate constitution.

Not all of Peter's brothers went to the university. Bia, the oldest, was with me in the review course for the law exam, but he never took it. Hans went through an agricultural training program; Peter studied law in Bonn and Breslau. He was a member of the Bonn Preussen, a fraternity that he liked belonging to and who gave us a good meal on our honeymoon in Bonn. Among these fraternity brothers he found lifelong friendships: Dieter Dönhoff, Sylvius Pückler from Branitz, and Adolph Steengracht from Moyland near Kleve.

Hans was killed in action in September of 1939. His mother reacted to his death like a mother in a classical tragedy. She was completely beside herself that her beloved Hans, for whom she had lain in bed for seven months during pregnancy, was now dead. We immediately called in Dävy from Wernersdorf, for she was the only person who could talk to this despairing woman.

Dävy had already taken care of her when Peter's father died quite suddenly in 1923. She had gone to bed and didn't want to get up ever again. And not until Püzze got typhoid fever did her motherly feelings reawaken, and she took care of her. When in 1943 the youngest son, Heinrich, was killed, she was already much calmer. She had just written to him when this news came. "Oh," she said, "I am very near to him." Then she became very quiet and didn't have those archaic outbursts as with Hans.

But back to the two of us. Fourteen days before the wedding Peter took the licensing exam. He had fixed the date so that he could get married in peace, even if he should fail the exam. . . . We had a church wedding in the Schleiermacher Kirche on Kaiserhof in present-day East Berlin. It was all tremendously festive. You know, it is just this kind of thing that one keeps in one's memory rather than the depressing things. Memory is more inclined to show everything in rosy colors, at least with me. And when people say about me that this woman has surely lived through a lot, then I must answer that even the terrible things are and remain a spiritual treasure for me, one that I would not like to do without, and from which I still derive strength today!

Nevertheless, for me the wedding was not the most important thing in my life. For in the evening, I was unhappy. I thought, now I am simply letting my father go home, and I still belong with him too! It was for me an almost sad idea that I now had to stay with my husband. . . .

Stubborn as we were, we wanted to furnish our apartment on Lützowufer ourselves, and consequently it looked at first like a disorderly junk store. There was a mattress, I think, and a wonderful old bed, and nothing else. In the meantime my sister-in-law Dävy Moltke had come and had at least cleaned up, had laid down a rug from Constantinople (where her husband was a diplomatic advisor), had put up a lamp, and made the beds. So it looked almost cozy, and we were very thankful to her for that. But otherwise there were boxes full of books sitting around, and

Peter and I actually began to unpack immediately, in the middle of our wedding night. And little by little the apartment became prettier and more comfortable.

We did not have a financial nest egg at that time. Peter had given a friend in need a large part of his fortune—he had done that without hesitating for a second. In that way he was splendid. But because we had almost no money ourselves, he soon had to look for a job. At first he worked in the law practice where he had worked as a law clerk, and we still lived in this wonderful apartment on Lützowufer into which we had moved after the wedding. But soon, in fact at the end of 1931, the rent became too expensive, and we moved into a gloomy courtyard apartment on Ansbacher Strasse at Wittenbergplatz. This apartment belonged to our painter friend Luckner—a great-grandson of that Luckner to whom the "Marseillaise" is dedicated! We sublet our own apartment to a Norwegian friend. But even in this small, dark, two-room apartment we had a nice time. I cooked for Peter and for Luckner, who was a very good friend to both of us, and I still have many of his pictures. And sometimes Luckner would call me and say, "Come on over and take a look at the picture." And then I would run over to his place, but usually came back quickly because Peter liked it when I was home when he returned. Once when it got late, the porter stood on the street and said, "Do come home, Countess!" In fact Peter, when he had seen that no one was there, had loudly slammed the door and was gone. This porter was actually my first encounter with a dyed in the wool Berliner. He was a great fellow with protruding eyes that almost popped out of his head. Often he knocked on the door in the morning and said, "Where is the trash can? When shall I wash the windows?"

We just didn't have very much money, and sometimes we ate only potatoes or carrots. Whenever Peter or Luckner did get money, they put it in the so-called silver ship—that was a cigar box. For during the great economic crisis Peter received his salary not in bills, but for the most part in silver coins and pennies; all that was poured into the silver ship. Often I would then go quickly to the Kaufhaus des Westens, the KaDeWe, and do my shopping. Once there was so little money that all I bought was a roll of toilet paper and a little bouquet of violets — which, I thought, were the most important things. But we weren't hungry, and we weren't unhappy or worried about our tight finances. Whenever things got really bad we went to Kleinöls or Kauern, and I brought back a lot to eat.

I still remember that Püzze Siemens, Peter's eldest sister, once visited us in the Berlin apartment and said, "You're really living high on the hog here." She was quite envious, for she felt that her own big house was a burden. She had four children, a big garden, and many servants; everything was carried out on a grand scale, but it strained her. She especially took the raising of her children very seriously. But in spite of that she still could have done something else too. She was an intelligent woman, and I always admired her. She was incredibly quick-witted. Once a cousin got married and visited Peter's mother with his wife. All those who were at Kleinöls at the time were sitting together. This woman did not have the good will of the family, but everyone was fairly civil; only Püzze said not a single word. Afterwards the family reproached her and said, "You should have . . ." and "That wasn't very friendly of you. . . ." She answered only, "Better an afternoon of being unfriendly than a life time of being related." To Peter and me she once said, "Oh, one need not worry about you two — you can live just as well on a train track as in a palace."

Püzze was born in 1899, but after the war she always said it was 1900. She wanted to be born in this century, and since her birth certificate got lost in Silesia, she simply maintained that. Even after the war she had an astonishing life, because the Americans appointed her one of the advocates for displaced persons here in Berlin. In a truly sacrificing manner she ran about and looked, went to America, to Italy, wrote everywhere. Everywhere she reestablished the connection to the world for displaced persons and concentration camp survivors who had been dragged off by the Germans; and she did all that without a secretary, typing everything herself, without a chauffeur and without a car. Her husband was Friedrich Karl Siemens, a cousin of Karl Friedrich Siemens. He died shortly after his wife in 1953. How appalled she would be, if she knew that her truth-loving husband had put the correct birth date on her grave stone!

We lived on Lützowufer from around 1930 till the new year of 1931–32. In the first years of marriage our "togetherness" fulfilled us, and we actually had only a few friends, but we had a large family that kept us quite busy in our free time. Otherwise we were mainly friends with the painter Luckner I mentioned, but also with some others such as Hermann and Inez Abs. Among our good friends there were also men of poetic sensibility like Martin Katte, for instance, for whom the current political matters were of little importance but who was firmly rooted in his homeland, which had both an aristocratic and a peasant tradition. We frequently visited him and his wife Anne at Zolchow, their beautiful estate in the Chatte corner of western Mark Brandenburg; here there was an atmosphere as in Fontane's *Stechlin*. Our trips to Silesia were also often interrupted in Branitz in the Lausitz with the Pückler family, where we could forget the daily routine. Nevertheless, we didn't have then such a social life as I have now. In the first years at Lützowufer we went to Silesia as often as possible. Of course we met friends and acquaintances in Berlin at exhibitions or concerts, but that was really all. You know, such a big family often takes the place of friends. Here in Berlin, Püzze and Dävy also lived with their families. Then Peter wanted to change his job. The lawyer with whom he worked was active in the real estate sector, but Peter didn't want to do that for the long run. He found a position for a short time with the Eastern Relief, where again he earned very little but could do a lot of travelling. He had to visit the estates that had gotten into financial difficulties and were supposed to receive help. As mentioned, I worked for a while for a lawyer, but really I wanted to have children. And it is probably not a favorable precondition when one wants them no matter what the cost. I kept having to go to the spa, to the Bohemian Franzensbad, to Bad Elster, for all sorts of examinations, but everything seemed in order. Peter's mother of course longed for a grandchild; nevertheless, I was thankful to her and Peter, that they never pressured me on that account. I once had a miscarriage, and Peter said only, "You know it is not just your sorrow, it is our sorrow." He could fulfill his life even without children; he also wrote that in his last letter.

Professionally speaking, with the beginning of the Third Reich, every possibility was closed to me, except for a position as a lawyer. Women were not allowed then to become judges, and in the meantime the exams and the legal world were far behind me. I later worked for Kauern, together with my brother-in-law Hannusch. But I'll tell you more about that later.

On the day of the seizure of power, 30 January 1933, we saw the torchlight procession on Wilhelmstrasse. Peter had said, "Let's have a look at that," so we went to see it. For us it already seemed very eerie, but to people who were in great economic distress Hitler promised work, and help along with that, so one should probably excuse many people at that time for their honest belief in a better future. They did not suspect what a disaster Hitler would bring to all of us. Peter and I were standing in an excited crowd of people at the torchlight procession, and when the SA drew past with its marching step we felt this mass experience, which so repelled Peter that he was never even tempted to participate in it. He later spent half a year in the labor service because without it he could not get a position as a government civil servant. The labor service was considered a substitute for membership in the party. By the way, he liked to work there. He had to regulate the Havel with young Berlin workers' sons, and he got along well with them. They were good buddies and helped Peter with the difficult manual labor that he was not used to. It was simply very difficult to know immediately where that would lead. I did not read *Mein Kampf* at that time or any time afterward. However, I knew very soon that many people had been locked up. When Peter was still with the Eastern Relief—so already in 1933—we once went to Torgau and traveled past a camp that was fenced in with thick barbed wire, the lower part a big fence and above it barbed wire inside and out, and Peter said, "That is a concentration camp."

Such camps were built very soon after the seizure of power. I also still recall our horror over a newspaper article many years later, in which the subject was a telegram by Gauleiter Koch of East Prussia, who obediently informed his Führer that East Prussia was now "free of Jews." At that time we talked for a long time and in a larger circle about this horrible organized killing by Germans. His impotence when confronted with the crimes in the Third Reich tormented Peter the most. And for that reason he participated in the Twentieth of July. Not so much for political reasons, in order to kill Hitler, but rather to bring to an end this horrible murder of Jews and the war in general, whose consequences were, of course, not only confined to Germany, but were also terrible for the French, Norwegians and Dutch, Poles and Russians.

Sometime after the Röhm Putsch in 1934 Peter began to look for people who seemed politically and intellectually related to him. For example, he sat down with Ehrensberger, who was at that time an assistant secretary, and with Albrecht Kessel and others, and talked with them about questions of national law and foreign affairs.

Peter was, by the way, as I had been previously, more of an apolitical person. I cannot recall that we had ever spoken about daily politics before 1933. He was by nature more of an artistic and contemplative person. He liked to go to concerts and read a lot of literature, as well as history and theology. The Yorck children had been accustomed by their father to learning a lot by heart. Every night the father read aloud to the children at the level of the older ones, but the little ones were usually present and found this atmosphere cozy and sat under the table. Peter's mother once told me an early story about Peter: how he was also sitting on the floor, and suddenly his father, who was enormously worshiped, spat out some little hair, and it fell on Peter's head. And in the evening, when he was supposed to be washed, he didn't want them to wash off "the beautiful thing."

Peter read a lot of classics, again and again. They gave him a lot: it was not wasteful ballast for him. Once, for example, in the middle of the war, together with Helmuth Moltke and Eugen Gerstenmaier, we read *Iphigenie*. Peter could recite by heart the poems of young Goethe from his Strassburg phase and complete parts of *Faust*. When he was arrested I often thought how good it was for him that he had all that in his head. But he also read modern works: Rilke's poems, Ernst Jünger, who was much discussed then, novels by Hamsun. We did not yet have Kafka—I read him for the first time after the war—nor did we have Brecht or anything expressionistic. I got to know all of that only after the war. We saw mostly classical pieces in the theater. We were not curious about what was contemporary because only the classics were offered to us in their entirety.

He did not concern himself with family history: he was not interested in that. But he always enjoyed learning something about philosophy. His grandfather Paul Yorck was a philosophical thinker, but Peter never got to that. Around the end of the war he read, together with a colleague on the staff of the Eastern Relief, works by the theologian Holl, and he even wrote compositions; but that is all burned and gone. The closer the end of his life came, the more he asked about these things and was searching. . . .

Peter was obstinate, but also spontaneously generous. His father asked him once when he was four years old, "What do you want to be?" He answered, "A field marshal or a cook." The father said, "Both are difficult." Peter: "Well, I can at least try." And when he worked in 1931–32 for the commissioner for Eastern Relief, he came home one morning in his old Opel without a coat or shoes. He had given them to someone on the way, who, he said, needed them more than he himself did.

It is not a coincidence that Hortensienstrasse became the local center for the growing circle of friends and other resistance workers. For Peter was, with his level nature, the born mediator between such different men as his cousin Claus Stauffenberg, General Beck, Julius Leber, and his closest friend Helmuth Moltke. Peter had a pronounced ability to balance practical and personal differences in an honest way without cheap compromises. For him Prussianness did not mean a false military pathos, but rather always being ready to help others as a freedom-loving Christian.

3

WE LIVED IN BRESLAU from 1933 to 1936. Peter had a position as a government civil servant with the Oberpräsidium; we moved into a pretty apartment on Lindenallee and by now had a lot of visitors and acquaintances. You see, we had attended a course in general studies at the university, whose participants included not only Günter Schmölders, a national economist; but also Viktor Weizsäcker, a doctor; Peter Rassow, a historian; Friedrich Gogarten, a theologian; and many others. All the professors, as well as sculptors, painters, and architects, had formed a group, and every two weeks, as I recall, each had to give a lecture in his field—a kind of lecture series. But the nice thing was that there were not only the lectures, but also real discussions about them; each had listened to the other. At that time Peter did not feel exactly at home in this respected circle of professors, but he was a welcome guest.

Professors had, by the way, played a big role in the life of Peter's father. They often came along with their families to

Kleinöls, and more often than not the table was set for thirty people. The rooms in the so-called bursary wing of the mansion had the names of professors. Peter's father fostered that a great deal.

In Breslau I was also very happy in other respects. Maria, my dear Mariechen, about whom I want to talk later, already lived with us and cooked wonderfully. I befriended Etta Koenigs, of the Kalckreuth family, a cousin of Peter's, who was somewhat crazy but very musical and highly talented.

In Silesia we also had good friends in the country. We often visited the Praschmases in Falkenberg, in Upper Silesia. A wonderful old castle, a spectacular forest nearby that was full of azaleas, and when they bloomed, the fragrance was quite overpowering. Peter, by the way, regarded the Catholic nobility in the neighborhood more highly than the Protestant; even his father used to say, lovingly and derisively, that the Protestants were raised like simple cattle. The Kleinöls Yorcks were intellectually demanding people. They had a universal education in history, philosophy, and the arts, a cohesive strength that everyone felt who had contact with them. Most Protestants were preoccupied with hunting and their socially antiquated customs; they were narrow-minded, and Peter was bored by them.

Our closest neighbors were the Prittwitzes, and one of Peter's most beloved sisters even married a Prittwitz. But we never became as friendly with the other nearby and more distant neighbors.

From Breslau we went to Kauern and Kleinöls nearly every weekend. I can recall the Christmas celebrations especially well. At midnight the family went to the family tomb, a Schinkelbau, where Peter's father, grandfather, great-grandfather, and the field marshal are buried, and brought along small trees with Christmas lights. Afterwards Peter and I often went to Midnight Mass at four o'clock in the morning in the cathedral at Breslau. That was wonderful every time we went.

Kleinöls, or Klein-Oels, was an endowment to field marshal

Yorck in gratitude for the fact that he had brought about the crossing of the Elbe near Wartenburg on 3 October 1813. Six estates belonged to Kleinöls: Kauern, Weigwitz, Krausenau, Höckricht, Gaulau, and Bischwitz. They were all located some two to four kilometers from each other. During the time of the field marshal, his son lived in the so-called red manor at Kauern, an estate of twelve hundred acres. The estates were administered by inspectors and were all about as big as Kauern. All of it belonged to Bia, Peter's eldest brother. He transferred Kauern to his nine siblings for the purpose of settling debts. And with that Kauern became the basis of my brother-in-law Hans's livelihood. He had studied agriculture and now administered the estate. Peter and I had a small apartment there. When the war became menacing we took our nicest things there from Berlin: glasses, porcelain, the cabinets, everything that we had collected. Later I found the remains on the manure heap.

Bia was drafted and wounded in Italy by a shot in the shoulder; after the Twentieth of July he remained in jail until the end of the war. He had already been expelled from the party after the Röhm Putsch in 1934, and he later joined the Confessing Church. The church continued to remain an important part of his life.

My brother-in-law Hans had a good and intimate personal relationship with the people who worked on the Kauern estate. In the evenings he often went to one of the families and chatted with them: what the kids were doing, what they should perhaps some day study, whether someone was sick, what the ailment was, and so on. All of that was patriarchal and trusting in the best sense. The establishment of a kindergarten was a progressive idea and something quite special. Earlier, child care had been the old women's task. What the older children did outside of school concerned no one. Like mother doves, the old women fed the babies by chewing bites of food that they then pushed into the babies' mouths. Certainly, that was not exactly hygienic, but in spite of that the babies were not sick often. With children, though, there was often the danger of diphtheria.

So Hannusch was very popular, and Peter and I inherited that favor. After Hannusch was killed in action in the first days of the war, and I had taken over the administration, I could still bask in the affection toward him. Another reason that I took over the administration at the end of 1942 was because otherwise, as a childless woman, I might have had to work in a munitions factory. So in Kauern I became the lady of the manor, so to speak, in collaboration with our long-standing Inspector Lampl. What I had previously done occasionally with my brother-in-law, I now did alone. I had to make sure the wheat was treated for virus, and so on, but I didn't really have to *do* much, because the inspectors and workers understood much more about the matter than I did. But I had to *be* there.

Besides keeping the books, my main task was to make decisions when asked. For example, we discussed such things as when the summer sowing should begin, or when the carrots should be planted. Together with the inspector I listened to the opinions of the workers, and then we made the decision. In fact, we always had good luck with the harvests. One had to have luck because much more happens in the country than in the city: either something or other gets broken or animals get sick or barns have to be plastered or a roof has to be replaced and so on. For example, the big wonderful sheepfold, in which two hundred and fifty ewes were housed, had to be renovated once. And thus there were almost always bricklayers, tractor drivers, and cartwrights working on the farm. There was also a master shepherd. Those are great men, with a special reputation and standing. The ones I got to know were quiet people who understood their subject very well. Because for a herd such as ours of approximately 250 mothers and 6 rams to thrive, the shepherd must have a close relationship to the animals. He has to help them with their births and care for the lambs, always quietly and carefully.

All in all on the estate there were about sixty children, whom one had to know by name, from eighteen or nineteen families. Among them were several so-called Stellenbesitzer, who did not live directly on the estate, but rather had their own house and a piece of land. This land was plowed along with the estate and harvested by the owners.

In Silesia a lot of beets were grown; they were valuable and really brought in money when the harvest was good and the sugar percentage high. Beet cultivation was a difficult job. For first of all there was no machine for hoeing—the beets were sown and later thinned by hand, and then hoed two or three times before they were left to grow on their own. Women did all of that. All in all I have to say that on the land the women worked harder than the men, who it's true led the ox and horse carts but didn't have to hoe. That is a very strenuous job. Today there are finally machines for that. At that time older women sometimes looked completely horizontally bent, so curved was their spine. Then they still had their children and their own livestock to take care of! For each family had chickens and a few ducks or geese and at least two pigs.

The men were needed to load the beet harvest and to drive to the train station with the carts. We had about eight or ten carts at Kauern with big horses, for then there were of course no rubber tires. And I recall that sometimes the carts with the harvest sank so deep into the ground that they could only be pulled out with four teams.

Beets, like wine, get the best amount of sugar in the fall. One harvests them at the end of September or the beginning of October, but one has to be careful when the frost comes too early. Besides beets, we cultivated wheat, oats, rapeseed, potatoes, and peas at Kauern. So we had little cattle business. Hannusch was especially interested in the fields, in green manuring, for the fields soon become tired of the beets, and then one has to care for them and enrich the soil. Often one cannot plant any more beets for many years but rather must do something else.

Grain was first harvested with combines at Kauern and then put into the granary, where unfortunately there were always rats. There it had to be constantly turned so that it would remain dry.

When the old grain was sold and the new still maturing, the milk business brought in the necessary money. I know from the figures that the last wages in June and July, for example, were coming from the milk business. That tided us over. We were connected to a central dairy; the milk was picked up—we could not sell it ourselves. But everything was still milked by hand, by Duckschen [1] and two other women.

The people were opposed to wages. They had their gardens and their livestock, with which they could do what they wanted. They did not have to pay rent. Above all they always got their payment in kind in the fall. That consisted of milk, corn, potatoes, sugar, linen, rapeseed. The payment in kind was stored in the granary, and each got his share. Actually there was no theft and no complaints that one got too much or another too little. The payment in kind of grain and so on was stored centrally, because the people simply had little room and many children. There were new houses for the workers—very nice homes, for four families—but most lived in the manor that had been renovated for workers in the last century.

Whenever the people were sick a compulsory workers' medical insurance plan kicked in for them. For the old people, a nice home had been built in Kleinöls, because at home it usually became too cramped for them and such old folks were often grumpy. Pretty rooms had been furnished for them, but they wanted to go back to their families and so they all went home again, one after the other. They were so unhappy, and I could understand them. We then tried to house them in built-on or empty rooms at the farm. In exchange the old people watched the children and helped out a lot in other ways. So no one actu-

1. A worker at Kauern responsible for the dairy cows.

ally retired from public life. They often sat at the farm, on a bench in the sun, relaxing and watching whatever happened to be going on.

I still remember the death of old Gottlieb Gebühr, who for decades had led the oxen. Leading the oxen is a tremendously slow matter. An ox has a pace half as fast as a horse. And old Gottlieb walked exactly like that anyway. He got sick one day with cancer and died. He was laid out with many flowers in a barn, and everyone came. He was right in the middle of everyone again, and at the end there was a ceremony during which the casket stood open. Everything was photographed. Suddenly an old woman said to me, "What a beautiful corpse!"

Everything is just so natural in the country, even death. It tears open a hole no doubt, and so it was with Gottlieb for me; for although he didn't say much, he had humor, and the life rhythm he brought along was beautiful. Then he was buried and his wife took care of the grave without making a cult of it. It only had to be orderly. He was buried in Weigwitz—the church was also there. That was about two or three kilometers away.

The farmers were otherwise not very religious, and they also didn't often go to church. And Peter and his family only went to church for special celebrations. The school was also in Weigwitz, and the children went there on foot in the mornings. The teachers at that time were not only teachers: they could play the organ, usually understood something about bees, a lot about gardening, and about raising chickens; they were always a central point of knowledge in the village. Later we had two teachers. You see, there were many school children in Kauern and just as many in Weigwitz.

There were no Nazis in Kauern or in Kleinöls. Even the very strict and feared inspectors at the other estates weren't Nazis. One of the farms in the village belonged to the local farm leader, but even he was no Nazi, and he never betrayed us. He was a very good farmer, and so was Hannusch, and in that they were equal to each other. To illustrate that, I want to relate the following story. During the war they had assigned us Polish forced laborers, because the men from the estate had been drafted. The Poles came from the area of Krakow with nothing more than a little sack of possessions. Our people were amazed and asked, "Why did they leave their farms?" And I answered them, "We drove them away and put Germans in their place."

I treated the Poles exactly as I treated our people. They received the same payment in kind of sugar, of linen, of everything. They were, by the way, very clean people. Among them were two old women who did the cooking and all the washing for the group—perhaps six families. The girls came to the beet fields almost every day with clean stockings, and our people stared at that: this degree of cleanliness surprised them. One day one of these Poles—his name was Pjotr—suddenly flew into a rage. He went after a worker with a whip. Thank God he did not hit him in his fit of rage; he then threw the whip away and did not want to talk with anyone. That was early in the morning in front of the stable door, and there were many witnesses. Such a thing was easily reported to the Nazis. For that reason I greatly feared for his life and said, "Now we just want to stick together. No one will say a word about it. That can happen to any one of us. We will wait until the Count comes, then we'll talk about it."

No one said anything, and Peter came on Saturday. And the two Peters, Pjotr and Peter, walked for an hour and a half around this giant farm. In the middle was a small house, where the shepherd lived with his family, and also where French prisoners of war were housed. So the two walked in a circle around the farm and talked and talked. Then the worker was called as well as the other people, and Pjotr apologized in everyone's presence, and Peter said, "And now this is all over, now we keep quiet."

If Pjotr had been reported, he would have landed immediately in a concentration camp. That was around 1941–42.

In June of 1945, after the end of the war, I went on foot for the first time from Kreisau, the estate of the Moltke family, to Kauern, together with Peter's sister Muto. That is about a two-day march. On the way we met a man who had a kind of stick over his shoulder from which there hung a small bundle, and I thought, "I know him," and it turned out to be Pjotr. And Pjotr then helped Muto and me from that time on; he was our interpreter. And so we were in a good position with regard to the Russians, for he told them about Peter, so that no Russian did anything to hurt us; to the contrary, they even wanted to give us cows.

But that Pjotr, he really surprised me. All decent things that one sows, benevolent gestures, always come back, with interest. And so it was with Pjotr.

At Kleinöls and Kauern before the war there were big parties, above all, hunting dinners. Peter organized the hunts, although he didn't hunt himself. First of all there was usually a completely informal hunt for partridges, with only three, four, or five hunters. That was in September, and actually it was one of the nicest hunts, in part because the dogs participated with such excitement. For example, I still remember Asso, the one Gordon setter. Asso was downright enthusiastic. Whenever a bird is fired at, it hides itself, and the dogs sit in the beets, motionless. One only sees their eyes going back and forth. The dogs don't come back until they've found their booty. These fall hunts were so impressive because the Silesian scenery is the most beautiful in the fall: a sky that is very close, as during the harvest; it approaches a total blue and vaults much more than here and has a very special shine.

In Kauern we also went on excursions every year. These were business trips, so to speak, always after the harvest. We would rent a bus, and off we went. The whole thing ended up in a restaurant; we danced and drank. These parties were very enjoyable.

I still recall the story with Duckschen. In the cow barn we had about thirty milk cows; Duckschen was in charge—an exceptionally strong person, but utterly good-natured. Once we had traveled to the Eulen mountains. There Duckschen, completely overcome, screamed, "Look, there are mountains!" She had never seen any in her life. At that time traveling was almost unheard of. Even the nearby provincial capital Breslau was for most in the far distance. Where you lived you stayed, and actually quite happily and contentedly.

Among the farmers there were, I think, no celebrations other than the harvest festival. We didn't have Folklore or native costumes or such things. They didn't have all those German traditions as there were or are in Bavaria and the Black Forest. I also can't remember story telling. I only know that the old women liked best to talk about the family. They hung around closely together, and love for the family played a much bigger role than, for example, here in Berlin. They mostly married into the neighboring villages. That the daughter of a farm laborer should marry the son of a farmer was in itself hardly possible. But many girls were simply very capable, and with that you can convince some men! Anyway, that was my experience but admittedly nowadays, as a woman in a profession you still have to be better than the men. . . .

At any rate, at that time I was already traveling very frequently from Kauern to Berlin, because Peter wanted to have me around him more and more, and above all because it was there that ideas were gradually leading to preparatory actions for resistance.

4

IN 1937 WE MOVED BACK to Berlin, to Hortensienstrasse. Peter's boss Wagner, who up to that point was the president and Gauleiter of Silesia, was supposed to go from Breslau to Berlin as the price commissioner. Peter went on ahead to set up the offices, and Hortensienstrasse became our home until his death.

It was here that the bulk of the political activity of Peter and his friends up to the Twentieth of July was to take place.

A year after our move the Kristallnacht occurred. Peter and, especially, Maria were horrified. She became very, very quiet. What was hardest to bear was that it was impossible to express our opinion. We couldn't do anything. We were paralyzed with terror. So the only thing left to do was to search for friends and like-minded people, at least at first. At the time most Jews were rapidly going underground or emigrating if they didn't have an Aryan partner to protect them. But even if they had one, so I was told later, they had to clean up after bomb attacks on the S-Bahn and at the freight depots. They were put into crews with the Star of David on their clothes and had to work.

So it was now 1938, and Helmuth Moltke and Peter met for the first time. In fact, it was at the home of my sister-in-law Davida Moltke, on the occasion of a christening in Wernersdorf. Then in January 1940 Helmuth appeared at one of the first talks in Hortensienstrasse. This first meeting, however, was not very relaxed, but rather somewhat tentative—like a fencing match. First they had to become used to each other. But already in this conversation they staked out a broad range of questions. Then in a letter Helmuth recapitulated what they had in common and what separated them; Peter answered him, and in that way a correspondence between the two began, with the goal of clarifying each other's political views. Helmuth and Peter were very different. Helmuth had a dash of English character in his deliberate reserve. He was very straightforward, less artistic, and not only came off as, but also was, somewhat arrogant. Not toward simple people—he always dealt with them respectfully. He disliked any kind of boasting. He did not drink, was very precise in the way he organized his day, and was punctual to the minute. He also directed the conversations of the Friends, without allowing them to get off the subject. He was strong-willed, disciplined, orderly, and analytically intelligent.

Helmuth then also brought Eugen Gerstenmaier into our group. One or another of the group was always bringing along someone, saying, he's a good man, he understands the situation, and so on.

How did our apartment in Hortensienstrasse happen to become such a central place for the conspiracy? Helmuth used to live on Derfflinger Strasse, where he often invited individual guests for lunch. But later in the war he no longer wanted to sleep there because the house had a flat roof and was consequently very vulnerable to being bombed. After the first major air raid he moved all of his things to Hortensienstrasse—that was the beginning of March 1943—but he had already spent many a night at our place before. The impact from the bomb attacks in the neighborhood had torn the roof from our building several times, but it was only hit hard once, by a bomb that was destined for the S-Bahn at the end of our garden. We could still live in it though, and that was very important to us. We were completely focused on this home—we weren't celebrating in between attacks in the Adlon Hotel as apparently others were. And during these often regular evening meetings that the men attended we were so busy with political work that we didn't have time left for anything purely social.

Helmuth was, incidentally, a Spartan human being in his needs. He slept upstairs in a small garret. On his bed lay a sheet, and over that a wool blanket; everything was tidied up, even the bathroom that we all shared. He got up early and we didn't hear him at all. In the morning he already had the hot water for Peter's shave prepared and was making himself oatmeal. After he had been arrested in January 1944, the Gestapo came and said, "We want to take a look at the house where Count Moltke lived." The Gestapo men looked at the house and could only shake their heads, and one said, "And two counts with such names live in this house!" They probably were expecting a castle with down comforters. . . .

We never used the term "Kreisau Circle"; we called our group "the Friends." Freisler, or even before him the Gestapo, came up with the name, probably because at Kreisau, the Moltke estate in Silesia, there had been three meetings: one on Pentecost in 1942, then in October 1942 and once again on Pentecost in 1943. We met in the so-called mountain house, where we all found refuge after the Twentieth of July. But I'll explain about that presently.

The Kreisauers were not apolitical. Even though Fritz Schulenburg rather mockingly called the Friends a club of literati and aesthetes, it surely required a political sense to figure out how the constitution, the law, and education could be given their rightful place. "The act," in other words, the actual violent attack on the perpetrator of all this lawlessness, was initially rejected. But thinking about it and planning for the "day after" presupposed to a certain extent "the act," or at least the consequences of it. In any case, under the circumstances of the dictatorship, these discussions in and of themselves were indeed high treason and, contrary to Fritzi's mocking, already perilous.

We never knew just how many people to expect at each meeting of the Friends, and the meetings were hard work. The topics of the discussion were often proposed by Helmuth Moltke, and it was also he who frequently directed the discussions. He was the engine but, on the other hand, Peter was the integrating force, holding it together and balancing it. Furthermore, Peter had the connection to Stauffenberg. Although there were often weighty differences of opinion in political matters, everything came under the banner of our common opposition to the prevailing system, with the result that party politics in the democratic sense did not, and furthermore could not, exist.

Julius Leber was the one I remember in the most personal sense, though he did not directly belong to the group. I remember that Peter, Helmuth, and Leber met once for dinner at Hortensienstrasse. They wanted to cook, and each was supposed to cook a dish that he especially liked. Peter made an herb soup, similar to what was often served at Kleinöls; then came the main dish from Leber: wild rabbit in the Alsatian style; and Helmuth made little crêpes suzettes for dessert. Because we had to take great pains to keep Leber out of danger, he never actually met with the other friends at our place. However, there was a strong relationship of trust between Leber and Stauffenberg through Peter. Something really clicked between them. I always thought that you could read Leber's well-lined face like an open book. He was a skeptic toward people, but he wasn't bitter. He was older than Helmuth and Peter, and of course the long time in the concentration camp had left its mark. But he almost never spoke about it at all. Only one time he told me that in the concentration camp he had to lay himself over a vaulting horse, like the ones used in gymnastics, while a twenty-year-old SS man hit him on his exposed behind. All other forms of torture, for example, standing for hours in the hot sun, did not hurt him as much as this humiliation at the hands of a young man.

He wrote charming letters to his wife; he loved her above all else. But he did not take her quite seriously: she was a beam of sunshine to him and a little bird and other things like that. She did not know about the conspiracy until very late. He wanted to protect her. But of all of us women she probably had the worst fate because her husband was in a concentration camp for so long—I think it was five years all together—only to be killed at the end. And years later their son took his own life.

Claus Stauffenberg was from Lautlingen in Württemberg. He was a very kind and lovable man, and he always listened attentively to people he was speaking with. On the other hand, he was very determined, and very handsome besides. And yet he had lost an eye due to a bad wound in Africa, which had gravely damaged one half his face, and he had also lost the thumb and index finger on his right hand.[1] He was an extrovert, quite the

1. Stauffenberg had actually lost his right hand and two fingers on his left hand.

opposite of his elder brother Berthold Stauffenberg, with whom he had a close relationship. Both spent several years in the Stefan George circle. Their uncle Nikolaus Üxküll assumed the role of father for them. He loved the brothers like sons, and he was their model. Stauffenberg and the rest of us often met at "Nux's," as he was affectionately called. Ulrich Wilhelm Schwerin was also one of Stauffenberg's friends, and therefore one of ours too.

Then there was our friend Eugen Gerstenmaier, who even ended up living with us, and who at the time was rather young. He admired the Friends and, as counselor of the consistory, was specifically responsible for ecclesiastical matters. We valued his brilliance. He was fortunate enough to survive, and after the war he was a good, helpful friend to the whole, large conspirator family. After his sentence he wrote me a letter from the prison in Bayreuth that was filled with faith: "Deus est und Deus est pro nobis."[2]

For his part, Peter was more inclined towards the Catholic expression of Christianity. This was already evident during our Breslau time and was also apparent later through his close friendship with the Jesuits, especially with Father Delp, who was an amazing man. Viktor von Weizsäcker once said in this regard, "Well, you know, one must be born Catholic; one cannot become Catholic." However, Father Delp was someone who became Catholic. He converted, and in fact, rather passionately. Carlo Mierendorff was more of an artistically inclined man, who preferred most of all to converse about the theater and concerts. In those situations one would always notice how Helmuth became restless and would say, "Back to the subject."

We women did not stand aside through all of this. Peter never kept anything secret from me. I always knew when he was gone,

2. "God is and God is for us."

1. Marion Yorck at Kleinöls, about 1940

2. Top left: The Kleinöls manor
3. Bottom left: The Kauern estate
4. Above: Peter Yorck in 1938

5. Above: Hans Yorck ("Hannusch"), on horseback, 1937

6. Left: Irene Yorck ("Muto"), about 1940

7. Right: Peter Yorck before the outbreak of the war in 1939

8. Top: Peter Yorck before the
People's Court, 7–8 August 1944

9. Bottom: Marion Yorck in
the garden at 50 Hortensienstrasse

10. Top left: Maria Krause ("Mariechen"), about 1974

11. Top right: Marion Yorck as presiding
judge at a grand juvenile court, about 1965

12. Bottom: Ulrich Biel, about 1975

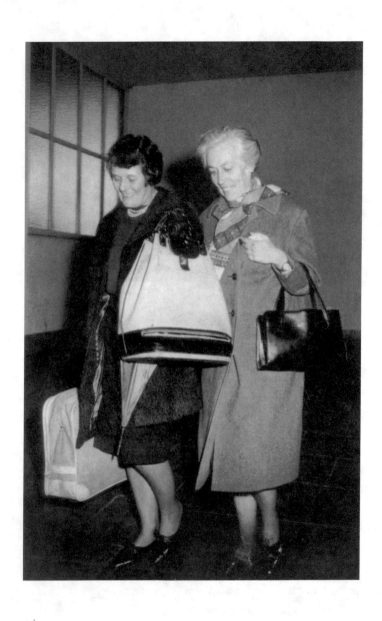

13. Marion Yorck and Freya Moltke
at Tempelhof Airport, about 1962

whom he was with, and how and when he intended to return home. He told me essentially everything. And I also took part in those discussions when I was in Berlin. I often cooked for the men, and was one of the group. I also had to deliver messages, several times to Leber, who at that time lived in Schöneberg, on a street that is now called Leberstrasse, at a coal merchant's with two exits so that he could disappear in an emergency.[3] We never telephoned Leber, nor Carlo Mierendorff. That's why I always went to Leber to make the appointments. These of course were simple assignments, but they had to be carried out. Freya Moltke was also well informed, mainly by means of Helmuth's letters, all of which have been preserved. To this day I have remained very good friends with Barbara Haeften, the sister of Klaus Curtius, who had been a fellow student of mine. Barbara played a big role in my life. Her husband, Hans Haeften, was a devout Protestant, a sensitive man who suffered deeply under the horrors of the Third Reich. He and Bärbel had already belonged to the Confessing Church since 1934. Hans, by the way, had also reflected for a long time on how to make the Protestant service livelier, so that the sermon alone would not be the focal point.

I have in fact the sense that Peter and Helmuth and Adam Trott, and particularly Hans Haeften and all the others, could not have done everything they did without their wives. All of them, after all, were dependent on their wives for love and companionship. And for provisions! For of course I was always dragging along suitcases full of food from Kauern. Sometimes eighty eggs, on which it was not a good idea to sit. These actions weren't without danger; the trains at that time were packed. I still remember that I sometimes stood for five hours with the suitcase between my legs. And once a soldier on whose shoulder I had fallen asleep said, "Why don't you just sit down?" "No," I

3. Leber had a coal business.

said, "I can't do that." "Oh," he said, "that must be something breakable . . ."

How people helped each other at that time, and how they understood one another!

I also brought along canned peas from Kauern. Every year there were eighty tins, and that was the work of the old women. They would sit under the linden tree in the courtyard and shell the peas. I also brought meat to Berlin, although everything at Kauern was actually rationed. The "annual pig," for example, was only allowed to weigh one hundred and twenty-five kilograms, but it actually weighed three hundred and fifty. When the meat inspector came after the slaughter, he wrote down "one hundred and fifty kilograms." Of course, he got his share for his trouble. So we didn't go hungry at Kauern, and we could still afford to give a lot of it away!

Among the women whom I knew there were hardly any Nazis. I know that many women enthusiastically voted for Hitler, and I can only explain it to myself in terms of the beginning of an emancipation. Hitler honored women; he bestowed the motherhood medals on them and arranged vacations for them. Of course, they were not allowed in professions; they had to stay with the children and in the kitchen but not in the church—instead of that there was the National Socialist Women's League. I did not meet my first real female Nazi, one who remained unrepentant after the war, until I was a judge. She was sentenced for crimes against humanity. During the war she had denounced a world famous ornithologist, a friend of hers from childhood, for a single defeatist remark about the war being already lost; because of this, Freisler sentenced the ornithologist to death. At the time of the woman's trial, I was a member of the court, and the presiding judge was Judge Levi, an old, clever, and wise Jew, almost like Lessing's Nathan. At the end he said quite shaken, "So, that still exists today." He himself had an Aryan wife and was thus able to survive. From my immediate surroundings

I can only think of one single woman who was devoted to the party. She lived on our street and collected things for the NS–People's Welfare, and she wanted us to subscribe to the *Völkischer Beobachter*, which we did not have. She was suspicious, we were too. She lived three houses down the street; we greeted each other, but that was all.

I only saw Hitler himself on one occasion, and that was at the Philharmonic. Furtwängler was conducting. I saw Hitler come in as the last patron, with his whole entourage of people around him, and sit down in the first row. I never heard him talk, not even on the radio.

In spite of everything I was never really afraid. Just once, on 17 January 1944, when the Gestapo arrested Helmuth Moltke.[4] We never anticipated that. And he also had not told us that he had warned Kiep, the former Reich press secretary who belonged to Mrs. Solf's group, about the surveillance of his telephone. Kiep was arrested, and he named Helmuth during the interrogation. So there we sat with Eugen Gerstenmaier and waited and waited, for Helmuth was always a very punctual man. And suddenly Eugen came from the room above and said simply, "They're here." And in fact two cars with dimmed lights stopped on Hortensienstrasse, which was noticeable as only a few people were still allowed to drive. Shortly thereafter two Gestapo men appeared. I still see the one in front of me—he had red hair and actually looked quite nice, at least not unfriendly; he would come frequently later on. They said to me: We have a letter here from Count Moltke for you, we are supposed to get his things for him. And while we were speaking with them like this, I tried to get out of them when and where they had arrested Helmuth, and where they were holding him now. We knew that he had had an appointment with Leber, and I wanted to find out whether Leber had also been arrested. But they just said: He is

4. The date was actually 19 January 1944.

well cared for. In the letter it said, "I am at Prinz-Albrecht-Strasse; please pack my toothbrush and the like, and tell Freya what's going on." Prinz-Albrecht-Strasse was the headquarters of the Gestapo. So on this night when Helmuth was arrested, Peter and I spoke a lot about ourselves, how much strength our togetherness gave us, and what we ought to do next. We slept very little, for this was the first time that we had had these characters in our house! For until this point the Gestapo actually had not suspected us. Now, however, they began to search, had us show them this and that, and were surprised that Helmuth had lived with us. They often came completely unannounced and went to the bookshelf, and I was always worried that some note or other, which Peter usually used as bookmarks or reminders, would fall out of the books. They acted as though they owned our apartment but without threatening us. Peter was not interrogated until his arrest.

In fact it was Helmuth Moltke who was against the Kreisauers participating in assassinating Hitler. He was of the opinion that only the military could carry and use weapons, that it was a matter for the generals. When he was arrested in January 1944 there was, I believe, not yet a firm date for the assassination attempt. At least I did not know of any. It was not until the beginning of July that I learned about the planned date, and that only after Leber and Reichwein, who had sought a contact with the Communists, had been arrested. Stauffenberg was worried that they would not be able to keep silent in the interrogations by the Gestapo and under the torture. He felt obligated to Julius Leber to try to do something.

Peter also did not believe in a big military action with participation by the generals. Rather, he had complete trust in Claus Stauffenberg. Stauffenberg had assured Peter, not that further words of assurance would have been necessary—as far as I can remember that was around Christmas 1943—that he would always be at his side. And that's the way it was on the Twentieth of July 1944.

Peter and Claus were both imbued with the idea that Hitler had broken his oath to the people. For both it was a question of murdering a tyrant, and they did not deal with this question easily.

During the last few weeks Peter's mood was very serious and very sad. He read the Bible often, much more than usual. I don't know if he believed in the success of the assassination attempt, but he did believe that it had to be attempted. Perhaps he already sensed that he was going to die, and that's why he was in this mood, one that I had already observed with Hannusch, before he went to war. This preparation for death, this releasing of one's self from a world in which one lived and worked, and in which one is rooted with head and heart, must be a very painful process.

One day, shortly before the assassination attempt, Peter and I visited Adam Trott, who lay sick in bed suffering from gallstones, and who said in despair, "When this monstrosity of a Hitler collapses, he'll take all of us down with him." That's what the mood was like then.

5

ON 18 JULY 1944 we traveled to Weimar, where on the twentieth the wedding of Sylvius Pückler was supposed to take place. We stayed in a pretty, old hotel in front of which stood a beautiful old fountain on the square. At the party the evening before the wedding,[1] Peter gave a talk in honor of the bridal couple, but it was actually a talk to me. The bride was quite sad because she probably sensed that Peter was elsewhere in his thoughts. Not until later could she properly understand where.

It had been arranged with Claus that Peter, if he heard nothing, would have to be at Bendlerstrasse on the twentieth, at eight in the morning. He heard nothing. No telegram came. We

1. This traditional party is called the *Polterabend* in German and is attended by both the bride and groom, along with their friends and relatives.

walked through the park; it was a wonderful night and we took a look at Goethe's garden house and sat for a while longer on the edge of the fountain. Peter's train was leaving at two in the morning. He packed his things and said, "Now I really must go." Those were his last words. I still see him going down the stairs—it was a spiral staircase—and he waved. He was in uniform so that he could travel undisturbed. Then, for me, he disappeared. *He* saw *me* once more, namely at the trial. He told Pastor Poelchau he had seen me from the paddy wagon as I was coming out of the present Allied Control Council building on Elssholzstrasse, where the People's Court met at that time.

So he departed from Weimar at night and arrived punctually in Berlin, where, as arranged, he went immediately to the headquarters of the Wehrmacht on Bendlerstrasse, the OKW. I was actually not supposed to come until two days later, but I was uneasy. After the church wedding ceremony in Weimar I set off right away the next day, on the twentieth. Near Bitterfeld there were heavy air raids, and the train remained at a standstill in the middle of the track. It seemed as though we'd never get to Berlin; eight in the evening came and I didn't know whether the assassination attempt had been successful or not. No one in the train said, "Thank God, the Führer lives," or, "Oh, what a shame that he isn't dead," or such and such. It was frightening for me. I had left around ten-thirty and arrived around eight in the evening—that's how long the trip from Weimar took, which usually only requires a good three hours! The train was very full, and posters with the slogan "Careful, the enemy is listening" hung everywhere in the compartments and corridors. People did not speak with each other and they didn't want to get to know each other either. When I arrived the train station was jam-packed with soldiers, as it always was then. Maria, God bless her, had found out where and when the train arrived and brought the message from Peter that I should immediately continue traveling on to Silesia. She also told me that the assassination attempt had probably failed. We walked from the Anhalter train station to the Silesian train station and then sat the whole night on the staircase steps in the train station and felt grateful for each other's nearness. Early in the morning, at eight, my train to Breslau departed. There in the station hotel, where I wanted to pick up something else for Kauern, there already resounded from the radio loudspeaker: "Those criminals!" and that Claus, of course, had been shot immediately. Our "heavenly Führer" was therefore still living, and Peter had been arrested.

So I traveled from Breslau on to Kauern but went very soon from Kauern to Peter's mother at Kleinöls. She had already heard about everything. The administrator had told her that the attempt had failed; later she was taken into kith-and-kin custody.[2] That was actually a wonderful solution for her, for in that way she had the feeling she could do something for Peter and didn't have to suffer his death as powerlessly as she had Hannusch's in 1939.

It was almost as though Hitler was not supposed to die. In that time period he was very careful in general, and he worked almost exclusively underground in Wolfschanze, which was dug two stories deep into the ground.[3] There the bomb would have actually destroyed everything and everyone! But on that day of all days, a beautiful day, he decided to hold the meeting in the hut![4]

In thinking about the time between 20 July and 7 August, the day of Peter's trial, I was always traveling. Several times I went back and forth between Berlin and Kleinöls and tried to get permission to visit Peter at many different departments of the Gestapo in Berlin, on Meineckestrasse, the Kurfürstenstrasse,

2. Under "kith and kin custody," relatives of the accused were also imprisoned.

3. This is a myth. In the swampy lake region there were no underground buildings.

4. This is another misconception. From 14 July 1944 on, all the meetings took place in the hut, and Stauffenberg knew this.

the Prinz-Albrecht-Palais—always in vain. The investigations were carried out on Meineckestrasse by a man by the name of Neuhaus, who, as I later heard, was a clever Protestant theology student. He looked at me at the first office call and declared, "You knew everything." I answered that I had lived and worked in Kauern and that Peter was by his nature much too discreet to talk about such things.

The trial before the People's Court under the chairmanship of Freisler took place on Monday and Tuesday, the seventh and eighth of August 1944. Dävy was willing to accompany me to Berlin. A friend took us only until Brieg, but he had such fear that he could be seen with the wife of that man that he let us out on the edge of the city. We then galloped the rest of the way to the train station. The train departed at midnight; it was the only one in which we knew that there was still room—the others were always all packed. Then we traveled to Berlin and stayed here on Im Dol with my sister-in-law Püzze Siemens. I could not go to Hortensienstrasse as the house had been confiscated. Later the Gestapo moved in. But at that time no one yet lived in it, and there was only the Gestapo seal stuck on the lock. So early on Monday I went to the People's Court, which at that time still met in the Superior Court of Justice building in Kleist Park on Potsdamerstrasse. I knew the building well from my time as a law clerk. There I spoke with a police officer and said, "These proceedings are also directed towards my husband, he is also accused. I would very much like to listen and see him." He looked at me, shook his head and said, "I can't do that, one only gets in there with very special permission." (By the way, Helmut Schmidt was allowed in as an observer.)

Then the police officer said, "But you can sit here," and took me along into the officers' room. There I only heard continually this dreadful voice of Freisler. In the films, you know, it was toned down. But I heard at that time nothing but this shrill, evil voice. He shouted down the accused in a cutting tone. They were hardly allowed to open their mouths. He already knew everything beforehand. A couple of times during the proceedings the police officer came to me and said that now it was Peter's turn.

These police officers left me there and not one of them said, "Your husband, this criminal, what are you thinking anyway?" Never did anyone say that. To the contrary, I felt their sympathy, which they were not allowed to express. When later, after my arrest, I was brought before two SS people because they wanted to photograph me for the rogues' gallery, one of them asked, "Your name?" I answered, "Yorck." He looked at me and said, "Please be seated, Countess." So even here there was the possibility of showing the respect that was meant for Peter.

So the trial proceeded, but my husband's defense lawyer, Bergmann, an old man, had not *once* been able to speak to Peter beforehand. He said in the main hearing he could not ask for leniency and mercy. The police officer told me that. Another defense lawyer of another defendant is supposed to have said to Freisler, "Give him the punishment he deserves." The defense lawyers stood before this court, if it could even be called that, before an insoluble task.

So during the whole trial I was next door in the police officers' room. The wives of other defendants were usually not in Berlin; they were evacuated because of their children and because of the air raids. Brigitte Gerstenmaier was in Mecklenburg with a sister of Eugen; Freya was in Kreisau but came repeatedly to Berlin to visit Helmuth in the concentration camp. Barbara Haeften was in jail; her children lived with her parents in Mecklenburg. Clarita Trott was in Gross Behnitz with our friends, the Borsigs.

Many wives were not at all informed. The men kept silent in order to protect them. They had to be very discrete anyway, and Peter was that by his nature. What he did not want to say, one didn't get out of him. Afterwards, the man who brought me to jail said to me, "Had we suspected that your husband knew so much we wouldn't have killed him so quickly." In this way Peter was probably spared torture, because the Gestapo believed he was involved in the assassination attempt only because he was the cousin of Claus Stauffenberg.

After the verdict had been pronounced on the eighth of August I ran once again back to Hortensienstrasse. I ran under a glaring sun through Berlin, and that was the only time in my life that I cursed the sun. I went into our house, for I still had the key, you see, and entered in spite of the Gestapo's seal on the lock. While Peter was dying I was probably on Hortensienstrasse. He died at six-thirty; I sat there until seven o'clock. I didn't know that he was dying. I thought about him and also prayed. I was completely calm.

Then I went to Im Dol, where I was living. Peter's sisters Püzze and Dävy and I each wrote one more letter to Peter. With these I then went from Dol on foot up to Prinz-Albrecht-Strasse, arrived there in the late evening and wanted to hand the letters to a Gestapo watchman at the gate. I said to him, "I would so much like for my husband to read these letters, he was condemned to death today, and I don't know how much longer he will live." And then the man said, "Just take your letters along with you. You know we are not brutes who carry out sentences in the evening." But by then Peter was already dead.

I heard from my sister Litta that Peter was dead. She called me the next morning. I wanted to ask her whether my brother had connections to people in the Third Reich, so I could see whether there was some possibility, but then my sister said, "You know, it's too late. Peter is dead."

The sentence was carried out on 8 August at 6:30 P.M. There was no grave. His ashes were scattered in the wind.

6

I WAS SUPPOSED to be arrested at Im Dol the next day, the ninth of August, a Wednesday. Actually, an arrest warrant had been issued at Kauern, but because I was continually en route they couldn't catch me in Silesia. Now, on the morning of the ninth of August, approximately four Gestapo men came to Im Dol to pick me up. However, I had already left early in the morning to see Pastor Lilje on Hortensienstrasse, in order to speak with him. I had not said at Dol where I was going. I didn't even know myself. I had just set off. I went to see Lilje—at that time he was still free—and we had a good conversation about Peter! It's true he hardly knew him personally, but I related that we had experienced a Communion with him, which Peter had written about in his last letter. At that time Lilje had laid his hand on the head of everyone who knelt down at Communion and had given him a quotation from the Bible. Peter's quotation was: "Fill me early with your grace, so will I praise you my whole life long."[1] This Communion must have been at the end of May or beginning of June, and Peter wrote afterwards in his letter: "It was almost like a call for me."

At that time Lilje was the secretary-general of the Lutheran World Convention, and also the secretary-general of the German Christian Student Organization. Before the war he had already made several trips abroad to America and India; he was a cosmopolitan, cheerful man, and he knew or was friends with the most important personages of the Lutheran Church abroad. He was a divinely gifted preacher for whom the sermon was really the center and main focus of the service. He always placed his sermon high above the events of the day; he lifted us up out of the despair over the horror of daily life. Later he himself was sentenced to seven years' imprisonment by the People's Court and was then freed by the Americans in 1945. Later he became

1. This is most likely a paraphrase of Psalm 90:14: "Satisfy us in the morning with your steadfast love, so that we may rejoice and be glad all our days."

the regional bishop of Hannover and the abbot of Loccum. So we spoke about Peter, and he then held a prayer for him in a small chapel of the church on Hortensienstrasse. He held prayers there every Wednesday afternoon. This time he spoke about the reading from the preceding day, 2 Timothy, chapter 4, verse 7: "I have fought the good fight, I have finished the race, I have kept the faith." There were many believers there—Lilje had a big congregation. No one knew that he spoke for Peter and me.

During this whole time the Gestapo had been guarding the house on Im Dol. They remained until the evening, and I still had not come home. Finally they left, and my brother-in-law Siemens gave his word to make sure that I would check in the next day at Meineckestrasse. I knew what that meant. "Meineckestrasse 10" was a Gestapo office. The building is still standing. When you rang below, a set of bars opened and then shut behind you. You went upstairs to the second floor, then some bars again closed behind you. So you could only go forward, not back.

I then spent a night at Prinz-Albrecht-Strasse, the Gestapo Headquarters—and that was the night of 10 to 11 August 1944—in a hideous cell with a door that was half-sized so that they could check whether the prisoner was standing or walking or lying on the bed. It was a sinister house.

The next day I went to Moabit, to a prison for those awaiting trial. I was there for almost three months. And you know, not being able to return to the lap of a very warm-hearted family was one of the most important experiences for me. I would have been loved and spoiled and would have had to speak a lot about everything. In Moabit, however, I learned what solitude is and lived as in a monk's cell. During this time I spoke to no one for almost three weeks, was not taken down for the walking rounds in the courtyard, had no work, and had nothing to read. So I locked everything up inside myself. Then I dreamed at night with such a liveliness that in the mornings I looked at the blue-checked straw mattress and asked myself, "Is that reality or the dream?" There was Peter, very near and speaking with me. I usually dreamed about Peter but very often also about my father. Once I dreamed that Peter's feet twitched in embers, and he had a completely enraptured appearance. Later I found a verse of Hölderlin, in which he says that the spirit is freed when the body is broken by physical suffering. This succeeds only when the human being is truly in extreme distress. But I didn't read that until after prison. Actually, Peter always looked happy in these dreams. Once he said, "You know, I was lucky again that nothing happened to me, but it was a close call." Curiously, in the dreams he then always retreated at some point. And when I tried to follow him—even when we were sitting together in the car and I wanted to look at him—I noticed how he disappeared. One of the last dreams was like a scene I later saw at the Portuguese coast: I saw cliffs extending on and on, and suddenly, quite unexpectedly, he appears, but at the moment I want to run to him and call, he is gone. Whenever I tried to touch him, he slipped away. I was not allowed to have him or to want to be near him.

I was interrogated only one single time while in custody. I was summoned in the evening. It was a small room; who interrogated me, I do not know. I denied everything. But when they put me in jail, I was actually ready to die. Harald Poelchau, the prison chaplain, had also asked me during his first visit, "Do you know that this may be your last stopping point in this world?" I said, "I know."

This time was so important precisely because I was so completely distanced from the daily routine, from my family, from my friends. You were able to keep everything locked up within yourself like in an oven: the togetherness with Peter, everything that affected me, everything that uplifted me, everything that I experienced. I was alone with my thoughts. Naturally, on the first day I ran like a caged tiger around in the cell. Since you cannot move, you feel like climbing the walls like the animals in the zoo. But that wears off later. Then you sit. The expression "to sit" is exactly right.[2]

On the third day, or after a week—in any event on a Wednesday—Harald Poelchau came. The door suddenly opened, and he stuck his head in. That was wonderful for me, as I had thought they were all dead! And now Harald came and told me that he had had a chance to pray an "Our Father" with Peter, and he said to me, "Do you know, I believe he did not lose the feeling of being a child of God." He also reported that Peter had had a chance to say to him that he had betrayed no name of the Friends.

Poelchau was actually the prison chaplain in Tegel. But because he had admittance to all prisons, they also let him visit us. In that respect the governess of the prison, whom I later helped with her de-nazification, was a wonderful person. For Poelchau came with bulging suit pockets, and in them were rock candy and carrots, honey rolls, and I don't know what else. He came every week, and he brought us everything, including letters, which of course was strictly forbidden. Often there were inspections afterwards, and once I thought, "Heaven forbid, what's going to happen now?"—because it was exactly the visiting day of the chaplain. For of course we didn't stuff ourselves with the goodies, because there was so little to eat. You put them away and divided them up for yourself. And there was this inspection, and I was afraid for Harald. But no matter who inspected, nothing turned up.

Looking back Harald Poelchau appears to me like a bridge between my life with Peter and my later one in the period after the war. He was the first who visited me in jail. Later, here in Berlin, it was he who was always ready with advice and help for all women and widows of the resistance. Clarita Trott's daughters lived with Harald and his wife Dorothee for many years while Clarita studied medicine in Heidelberg and the children

2. In German *sitzen* literally means *to sit*, but also *to spend time in jail*.

went to school here. I believe he helped shape the life and the character of these children. He was a man who was always ready to do something for others, and Dorothee was exactly the same. Their house in Zehlendorf was open to everyone. They had many close friends. He was a person who endeavored to be a Christian without making a show of it. He once said to me, "In Christianity what matters is the intention, the striving, and the effort, but not the performance." I see that also in my brother-in-law Siemens. Today one would call him an agnostic. In my memory he was someone who understood how to lead a truly godly life without the church. Harald Poelchau knew a lot about the resistance movements, but the Friends did not draw him in because he had other duties. He hid many Jews and other victims of persecution—not at his home, but he always knew addresses where it could be done. However, his main task was the spiritual well-being of prisoners, often up to their deaths. Years later he helped found the operation Sühnezeichen. He then traveled a lot and was often invited to Israel, always with his wife. They thanked him for his commitment. The conversations that Harald had with Peter and Helmuth before their deaths surely also left their mark on the farewell letters, at least concerning their Christian tone. He once said to me, "It is still with the Bible you can best help the people who must wait for their sentence to be carried out." In that way he was successful in conveying something, even with men like Theo Haubach, who surely didn't want to know anything about Christianity, and like Helmuth Moltke, whose thinking he guided in this direction. Finally it was also Poelchau who at the risk of his life smuggled all those letters out of jail. Had there been just one Nazi among the guards . . . but thank God nothing happened. By the way, Harald saw Helmuth Moltke every day in jail. After his arrest in January Helmuth was at first in the concentration camp Ravensbrück. Not until after Peter's death did he go to a Berlin jail. After the Twentieth of July Peter was in many different jails or concentration camps; the Gestapo feared a liberation attempt.

He was in Sachsenhausen, in Ravensbrück, in Berlin—almost every night somewhere else.

And then came the big surprise. One day, when for the first time I was taken for a walk in the courtyard, I saw in the cell next to me Bärbel Haeften, the sister of Klaus Curtius, with whom I had studied twenty years earlier. She sat there with crossed legs on her plank bed and sewed. We were both very amazed and happy to be near each other! But we didn't show it out of fear that they would separate us again. Bärbel had been arrested before me in spite of her five children and although she had just had her youngest daughter on 19 May. At the time of the arrest she was still nursing Ulrike, and despite that they arrested her and took her away from her child. Bärbel was at first full of despair, although she is really a pious person. Even today she has an amazing security in her faith. And so now we saw each other and, even though without words, could talk to each other. You see we found a very nice way to communicate with each other and to be together. The governess of the jail had given us a hymnal and a New Testament with the approval of the Gestapo. Of course, Bärbel knew all the songs much better than I did. And every evening, one, two, three, four, she tapped with her wedding ring on the pipe the number we would sing from the hymnal. And then we sang loudly. The walls in Moabit are tremendously thick. You didn't even hear it when someone went to the window and screamed. But we each knew that the other one was singing. Afterwards she would also tap out which Psalm we would read, and so we could communicate wonderfully, without any other person in the jail noticing it. Harald Poelchau taught us the tapping system.

In the jail there were also French women who had been drafted into forced labor and had been arrested because they refused to work. Very funny girls. I heard them in the evenings in the courtyard loudly singing the "Marseillaise"; during the day they continually came up with new hairstyles, which astonished the guards. And eventually the guards got angry because they could never figure out who was who. We called "bonjour" or "bonne nuit" to each other across the courtyard when we took our prison walk.

Later I got socks to darn: field gray socks that had been washed with bad soap and were completely hard and had gigantic holes. Bärbel Haeften knew how to sew on a machine, and she was allowed to mend old sheets and shirts. But we were most happy when Harald Poelchau came. He greatly overtaxed his strength and died in 1972. For us he always had this radiance when he came, even in his later years. I celebrated every New Year's Eve with him and Muto until 1950.

Then came the air raids, and because people like us were not "worth rescuing," as they said at the time, the women from the conspiracy circle were often moved together to the third floor. There we could see the light spectacle of the impending attacks when the English and when the Americans were approaching. But most of all we could talk to each other. That was unbelievably wonderful. The Gestapo naturally wanted to make us fearful by this transfer, but they didn't succeed. We weren't yet living again with our feet on the ground. It was also difficult after my release from jail. Of course it was marvelous that I could again get fresh air and breathe freely—literally speaking, for the air in the jail smells unpleasant, always like food and the toilet at the same time. That is the case in every jail; later as a judge I found it to be so.

As a judge I also once visited a crime scene at Moabit and met a guard from that time, who said to me, "Oh, those were the times when all the ladies were still with us!" These women noticed that we were different from the usual women who were there, even though I never considered myself to be a "lady." In any case, these female guards were often in bad moods at that time. I could see a kind of breakfast room through a small peephole, and when I heard them talking, I always thought, "Now who is actually free, they or I in my cell?" I learned that you experience true, deep inner freedom most strongly when outer freedom is gone. Only then. Then you notice what a gift it is.

Our guards changed continually. We thought, "Does that have to be?" They probably feared human relationships could develop. Again and again a new one came and inspected how we had made the beds, and each one had a different method. Many first tore the nicely made bed apart and said something like, "There, make it again, it's not right like that." That was a little bullying, but it didn't bother us. At least it kept us busy.

Our warden was a curious person, a thoughtful woman. She often came to see me; she had taken a liking to me. She told me later I had looked like a partisan from Yugoslavia with my long hair. One day she came to me and told me about Mädy Freytag-Loringhoven. Her husband had been a colonel at Wolfschanze, and when the assassination attempt failed, he shot himself. She lived in Salzburg and was probably an Austrian, had four children, and was picked up by the Gestapo in Salzburg and brought to jail in Berlin. She had no inkling of anything. And now the governess told me it was so bad with her that they would have to take her to Buch, a lunatic asylum as it was called then, in present-day East Berlin. She was going insane. She went wild in her cell, and they didn't know what to do with her. The governess had now gotten permission to ask me—before she took the woman to Buch—whether I would want to take her into my cell to help her. That was a human feeling. At first I was scared and thought about my wonderful solitude and quiet and said, "I don't know if I can do that, I don't know her at all." Then she said, "You know what, sleep on it a night, and I'll come again tomorrow morning." But already that evening I thought, "We are always talking about Christianity and compassion and here is a case, totally concrete, where I certainly couldn't say that my solitude is dearer to me than a distraught woman." And on the next day the governess came back, and I said the woman should come. Mädy Freytag-Loringhoven came immediately, hugged me, kissed me, was beside herself with happiness, and asked who I was, and talked without stopping. After about two or three hours I said to her, "You know what? Now we're going to make an agreement. Two hours of talking, three hours of quiet. Always alternating." But the first night was not good—it was very uneasy because she couldn't sleep. I saw her on that hard bed under the window and felt her restless movements. So I also couldn't sleep, and the restlessness of this person almost made the cell explode. On the next day I began with occupational therapy. You see, we had bugs. And I told her, "You know what, we are going to wipe the cell completely clean every other day, then perhaps we'll get the bugs out." The guard agreed to that. She brought us a bucket, and Mädy Freytag-Loringhoven was totally enthusiastic about being able to move and do something. Everything had been too much for her, above all because of her four children. The family had been torn apart and she couldn't cope with that. But this movement now, this being allowed to talk, was very good for her. I then explained to her what the Twentieth of July was all about, for she had no idea. She only knew about a failed assassination attempt, but she didn't know anything else. She also was not interested in politics. Not until later did they tell her that her husband was dead. Even her husband had never told her about what he was doing. But perhaps that was right in such a case. For when a woman with four children is pulled into such danger, without being able to do something herself, and then at the same time is supposed to preserve her innocence and lightheartedness in front of the children, that is almost impossible. She was, by the way, a very pretty and elegant woman and wore noticeably fine underwear. When she took off her dress and wiped the cell or washed her clothes, the female guards always looked on with big eyes. We had, you see, only one dress; we had no suitcases or anything, and you washed your clothes and then laid them under yourself during the night to dry. I think we otherwise only had aprons as prison clothing, grey sacks over our dresses.

Mädy Freytag-Loringhoven was released earlier than I. Then

I was transferred. The governess wanted to do something nice for me and put me in a cell in which the sun shone. In the cells on the second floor, where I had been up to now, there was a metal strip placed at an angle on the window sill outside, so that one couldn't see into the courtyard. I could only see the top of a small birch tree out the window, otherwise nothing, and no ray of sun came in. For that reason the governess had decided to put me in a sunny cell and moved me to the third floor next to the hospital. She probably also wanted them to give me something more to eat now and again, for I was quite thin. But in the new cell I was completely in despair. I was like a dog that was given a new doghouse, and I sat on the corner of my bed and thought, well, I don't want to put down roots here again. In the old cell I finally had become completely at home; I had my little cupboard and knew exactly what I could see, and Bärbel was next door. All of a sudden that was gone. I was completely alien here.

Annedore Leber and Clarita Trott were also in jail at that time, but I didn't know that. Freya Moltke and Romai Reichwein were never locked up; why, I don't know. Finally, after three months, I was released. Neuhaus, who as the Gestapo man led all the examinations in connection with the assassination attempt, commanded me at my release, "Don't go to Silesia, don't wear mourning, don't play the widow, and don't talk with other people about it." Those were the conditions.

Of course I said yes and went to stay with my sister-in-law Siemens on Im Dol. Later my brother-in-law provided me with three hundred marks, and then I immediately went to Silesia.

Peter's property had been confiscated in the judgement, so I had no money at all and also no longer any home here in Berlin—the Gestapo now used our house on Hortensienstrasse. So in spite of the ban I went straight to Silesia. I thought, "I have to go to Kauern." I wanted to go first of all to Peter's mother's house at Kleinöls. Then I got myself a horse and traveled in a small cart to Kauern. There, I drove in from the other side of the farm—through the back door, so to speak—so that my arrival would not immediately cause too much of a stir. There came the cartwright—actually a Communist, and in any case a proponent of class struggle—and the only one whom Hannusch and Peter had never quite trusted. And look now, he ran across the farm and said, "Good day, Countess, may I hold the horse?" I said, "Thank you." And then afterwards all the workers came to tell me how much they had admired Peter. But the Poles were the most sympathetic, the Polish women. They didn't say anything, but hugged me over and over and kissed my hand. I then called everyone together and said once again to them that they of course knew what had happened and that I was convinced that my husband, as a decent man, had followed his conscience.

They understood that, and no one held it against me; no one informed on me. They could have locked me up again, you see. The estate at that time was administered by our superintendent. In the meantime Peter's mother was also at home again; she had been held in prison for two months.

Now, a Gestapo man had told me that there was a long letter for me from Peter. I tried repeatedly at the Gestapo to get this letter. For that reason I went to four different departments in Berlin. The fourth time I came from Silesia to Berlin, in April 1945, because I'd been summoned to the Hotel Kaiserhof on Wilhelmplatz by an SS group leader. He offered me a pension. I replied that my husband hadn't died so that I could get a widow's pension. He thought for a short while, then he said, "Do you want his letter?" Finally I got it, and I traveled with this treasure back to Silesia. I then sewed it into a little linen sack and wore it on me during all my journeys to and through Silesia. It is written on war paper that has now almost completely deteriorated; the writing is hardly decipherable any more.

At the end of the war we could no longer remain at Kleinöls. The Front came nearer. We moved to Freya Moltke's at Kreisau, into the mountain house. The mountain house had played a big role in the Moltke family. It was not the manor. In the manor at that time there lived many refugees from all over, as well as friends like the Reichwein family. It is now rather neglected; the Poles let it fall into ruin. The mountain house up high was a charming house with thick walls and completely finished narrow garrets. There Helmuth had lived with his family for a long time. It was a harmonious country life with a big garden and an old superintendent.

At that time we were not evacuated, again because our lives were not "worth saving." So we remained in the mountain house, although some fleeing German soldiers told us, "Don't do that! The Russians are completely unpredictable." But we thought we had to face them sometime, and I still recall that now we were constantly waiting. Finally one day Freya came running and exclaimed, "I saw the first Russians!" She had seen a whole troop running across the fields; that must have been after the "Führer's birthday," so the end of April of 1945.

Sometime before the Russians came, it must have been the middle of April, I wanted to visit our people from Kauern in Czechoslovakia, where they had been evacuated. We couldn't go by rail, but we had bicycles, and with those my sister-in-law Muto and I bicycled through the Glatzer mountain area to the area of Königgrätz, and we were very hospitably received by the Czechs. These farmers experienced no hunger. Meanwhile they all had heard about Peter's fate. The Kauern people, whom we had sent there, were so popular that the Czechs kept them up until the end of 1946, because they did especially good field work. The Czechs had a wonderful small livestock breeding operation; I have never seen a goose like the one there, with sixteen small goslings! At our place in Kauern they had maybe six.

On the other hand, although the Czechs had well-tended fruit trees, the fields were full of weeds, and our people got rid of those, whereby they gained respect and were treated well. When Muto and I came completely by surprise, there was such joy among them! And we were literally stuffed every day.

Unfortunately, at that time I couldn't eat everything because right after my release from jail I had developed a bad case of jaundice. It lasted for months, and at the end my whole body was marbled, and I was repulsed by my own self. That was probably a physical reaction to everything that had gone on before. At that time my sister-in-law Dorothee at Kleinöls took loving care of me. I was, above all, not allowed to eat fat, so surely no fat goose like they offered us here in Czechoslovakia! It was just best to go hungry. In any event, in April of 1945 I talked seriously to the three mayors of the Czech villages, and they solemnly swore that they would care well for our people from Kauern, that they would not be tormented or chased away. Our people then stayed there and worked until an accommodation was found for them in the Eastern Zone.

Finally we pedaled back to Kreisau and saw, perhaps two weeks later, the first Russian there. He was a Siberian, a big strong fellow, who in the twinkling of an eye, took a pin out of his pocket, pricked open each one of our last fifteen eggs, and sucked it out, and the egg was gone. He spoke good German and explained that raw eggs were the best thing for men.

We also asked him, "What is to become of Silesia?" To this the Siberian said, "Stalin gave it to Poland." We had already suspected that for a long time.

Now there were three of us quite impressive women in Kreisau. Freya was very attractive, I was then once again quite good-looking, and Muto was as always; and now we were three women without men, which irritated the Russians a lot. "Where are your men?" they asked. "Partisans?" They always thought our men must be somewhere outside hidden in the potato fields, for it was by then the beginning of May, and the early potatoes already stood a little higher. But they found no men.

It was not so simple for us. They simply took everything they liked: radios, clocks, and so on. And for a period of two or three weeks, the women were also considered fair game, so to speak.

We had to hide ourselves from them, most of all at night. Often we had to escape to the cemetery at night, for they didn't dare go there. In that way we were spared. We also sometimes hid ourselves for days in the haystacks of the farmers, who lived further down. Freya suffered from migraines and had lice. But we usually had only a couple of days of peace, for by then the farmers were again in danger.

When the Russians wanted something from us, and they wanted everything possible, they called that *zapzarap—to take, to take* something pretty. It has somewhat of the meaning of our *klauen*,[3] but it is not meant as seriously. But then the thing was taken of course. When, for example, we were on our trips with a Russian and had a jacket on and also carried a blanket on our arm, then sometimes a Russian considered that to be too much and took one of the two away. But we knew that he probably gave it to someone else who, he believed, had no jacket or blanket. They shared everything with each other. I never saw a Russian eat when there were others in his presence who had nothing to eat.

Then in the early summer of 1945 Muto and I rode in a coal train from Glatz to Berlin and went to Hortensienstrasse. From there we returned several times to Silesia. We always crossed the Neisse illegally. Once we ran to Kauern to see how things were going there. It was the beginning of June 1945. Hardly anything had been cleaned up in the villages. I didn't see dead people there, but a lot of dead livestock covered with flies. Even our wonderfully white barn wall at Kauern was completely black with flies because so much decayed livestock lay around. Our house looked terrible. The Germans had established a hospital there; many simple wooden beds were still standing, and our furniture was gone. Only scraps of a beautiful carpet that came from my grandmother still lay on the dung heap. In the last vil-

3. To swipe or steal.

lage before Kauern we again met Pjotr, the one whom Peter had once kept out of a concentration camp. Pjotr then stayed with us the whole time and helped us a lot.

In Kauern we lived with the old farmer Karbstein, who had not wanted to leave his house along with the others. Again and again Russians came here—Tartars, who had broken off from their units, had found a couple of cows somewhere and then wandered as stray vagabonds through the countryside. Those were very strange human beings and not harmless, especially when they had been drinking alcohol. We once lived a good three weeks with Tartars who were Muslims and who said their prayers. Muto and I had a Russian dictionary; with that we could communicate a little, but it didn't always work. For example, at Farmer Karbstein's there was a piano, inside of which we had put our only clock. One Tartar already had five clocks and really liked to play the piano, and he sang beautiful songs along with it. Suddenly his eyes became very big: he had discovered the clock. I said, "But you already have five, and we have none." But he was overjoyed that he could now conquer the sixth.

I no longer remember exactly how Muto and I got to Silesia each time. I recall trips on full open coal carts in the streaming rain, hour-long waits at train stations, and short distances that you could cover by train or in Russian trucks, where you quickly and resolutely had to say yes or no when they asked if you wanted to come along. These trips were also not without danger. Actually, they were quite unsafe. I still recall that Polish marauders sometimes jumped down from the bridges into the open freight cars of the trains that traveled very slowly. They simply jumped on and threw everything off the train that the respectable Germans had taken along, and at the first opportunity they jumped off and collected their loot along the tracks. You could only protect your things by sitting down on them; you could literally take only as much along as you could "sit on."[4]

Sometimes we also went on a Russian truck to the next village and then climbed out.

Why did we cross the Neisse so often and visit the people in Silesia? It was simply because there were still so many Germans there. They were so happy when we told them, we'll come again! For these people we were immensely important. And for us it was a long farewell, and a beautiful one, deeply embedded in my memory. To be sure we had no papers, just a note from the Russian command here in Berlin, on which was written in Russian that Peter had lost his life because of the Nazis and that one should help me. That was of course very useful for us.

This period was actually one of my most wonderful life phases because of the complete independence. I had no duties, no home, no husband, no children, no identification card, no money; only a back pack in which there was just a pair of stockings or a little food in cans (which the American colonel Hohenthal in Berlin had given us), and besides that some cigarettes as barter currency. It was an exciting, wild, and completely immediate life in nature and freedom.

We walked hundreds of kilometers through this beautiful country in all kinds of weather. That ended in January 1946 in jail, because the Poles thought, "Why in the world are these women coming again, there must be something behind it, are they looking for gold or other treasures?" They couldn't imagine that we willingly came from Berlin to Silesia. But with all the Germans who were still there we always had the best reception. The women immediately made hot water and prepared a malt coffee. They gave us their bed and were so happy that

---

4. Marion Yorck uses the German word *besitzen* which means *to own, have, possess*. *Besitzen* is clearly related to *sitzen*, *to sit*. The origins of *possess* and *besitzen* both have to do with the idea that a person owned what he could quite literally sit on.

people from the Reich came, for you see they were cut off from everything, had no telephone, no mail, no radio, and they knew nothing.

Our last trip to Silesia went as follows: we had celebrated Christmas of 1945 at Hortensienstrasse, where we again resided, Freya, Muto, and I. We had received a Christmas tree as a gift, and things were all very cozy because Maria—dear Mariechen—had finally returned after a long separation. For the first time we again had beds with linens and real napkins, but this completely unfamiliar comfort disturbed me, for I found that life was not yet so far normalized that one could live in such a way. Also, we wanted to go to Silesia again right at the beginning of January, because we had arranged to meet with several people there. And we did that. We traveled on 3 January 1946 to Görlitz along with Pastor Zinke, who had previously been the leader of Caritas in Breslau and who wanted to spend the night in a monastery near Görlitz. When we said goodbye to each other he said, "'Til we meet again, over here or over there!" And then we went to Kreisau, where we had a base with a young Polish woman, who always gave us the feeling that we were coming home. This time we immediately noticed that we were being observed by Polish police. By the next morning a car stopped in front of the door and we were taken for "questioning." We were brought to Schweidnitz, and there we remained three weeks in jail. It was a hotel-like place—at least we had a room with two beds to sleep in—and we were interrogated for hours. We were always separated, by a Pole who understood German, although the transcripts that he prepared were written in Polish. Afterwards we received page-long transcripts, and I was asked to sign them, having no idea what was in them.

These interrogations took place at different times. Often during the day, usually evenings, very often at night. The Polish policeman questioned us in a small room. A clerk sat there, and a harsh lamp shone in our faces so that we couldn't clearly see the two men. The policeman wore a black oilcloth coat and had a bottle standing at the leg of the chair. I can only say that he was not unfriendly and was in no way crude or tough. However, we had to tell him in a tone of epic proportions where we lived in Berlin. That interested him above all. When he heard that Hortensienstrasse was in the American sector, he was amazed that we had come voluntarily to Silesia and came to the conclusion we must have hidden a gold ingot somewhere and were looking for it. Thus the interrogations. Of course we had to deny continually that we had any kind of relationship with the Americans, that we even knew an American, which of course wasn't true. Even the note that the Russian had written out for me about Peter's fate was for the Pole no reason to set us free. We were somehow booty with which he could still operate. How, he didn't know. He hoped that someone or other would appear and offer him something in exchange for our freedom. It was a classic hostage situation. When the interrogations were over, after many days with a thousand repetitions, this man said, "If somehow I can manage I'm going to America." That was a really astounding turn about for someone who had been conducting himself like a Communist!

But we still were not allowed to leave; we had to stay in our room. Thank heavens Muto and I understood each other well. It did not become boring for us—there were even books. But one day they transported us to Breslau. Why, I do not know. That was no longer as nice, for we were taken to a prison cell that was actually only meant for one person, and there were already three women in it, with only one bed. We were there for weeks. And we also had to work there. We were picked up in the evening and had to clean the cells of other prisoners. I especially recall one night when we had to clean the cells of Russians. I think they were deserters. In any case, I can still see a man in his cell in front of me: he had set up a makeshift toilet in a corner and had ripped open the sack with which he was supposed to cover himself and crawled into it because he was freezing, for at that time it was very cold. We were also freezing. In any event he looked like Papageno, full of straw and feathers. He looked at me completely astonished and said, "You German?" And I said, "Yes," and he answered, "Good." And at that point I thought, "Thank goodness, someone at least has had a good experience with Germans." I began to clean his cell, and as he watched he told me something about Leipzig, where he had worked. Apparently he had been a Russian prisoner of war.

It was rather difficult for us to clean these cells, for we had no tools whatsoever except for a little piece of wood and our hands. The Polish guards looked at us and wondered whether we could do it. In any case I cleaned the cell well while thinking about this man who, for all I knew, might not even survive in prison. After two hours' work (there were also other cells) the Poles said, "Now you can have water." But they said that only out of respect, I think, because we had done this work quite naturally as though we had spent our whole lives removing other people's dirt. Only for that reason did they lead us to a shower. For the first time in weeks we again felt hot water on our skin and received soap and a hand towel.

The three other women with whom we shared the cell were very different. One was an Austrian—I don't know how she had come to Silesia; at any rate, they had apprehended her with counterfeit money. She was a nice person and knew very good recipes by heart. So we exchanged cooking recipes, for when one is hungry thoughts of good food do help. In any case, we felt almost as though we were at a banquet.

The other woman was a Volga German, who could hardly speak German, and whose parents had come to Germany during the war. She was looking for them. Although I could hardly communicate with her, she was a charming person and gave the impression of a completely lost lamb in this world. When we lay on the bed—we always took turns lying two at a time on the single bed—she was always overjoyed at the human warmth around her.

The third was, I think, a Russian.

We also told each other many stories; Muto related a novella by Chekhov and I talked for days about *Anna Karenina*. In that way we five passed the time very nicely.

No one knew what the Poles wanted from us. They simply apprehended people and hoped to learn or get something from them. At the beginning they at least knew our names, but those were lost in the course of time. At the end Muto and I were simply called "Yarek." One evening the cell was opened and Irene Yarek was taken out. I was beside myself, for this togetherness with Muto had been the only thing that allowed us to experience the whole thing not only as bearable, but also almost like an adventure—the belonging to each other, this closeness. I rang and tried to make myself noticed. It was impossible. Not until hours later did someone come and say, "Mario?" They had probably looked under Mario in the men's section and only then figured out where I was. Then I was led to a room where I again found Muto.

That night we were taken to a train station and put on a train. We had no idea where we were being taken, whether to Berlin or to an old, empty concentration camp; everything was completely uncertain. The train went to Warsaw.

There we were taken to the headquarters of the political police, which was run by a Russian and a Polish colonel. The Russian interrogated us. He saw the note that the command in Berlin had given and said, "Good, I will help you. I will release you." I answered, full of fear, "But please, surely not *here*!" For I was worried that they would immediately apprehend us again and drag us I don't know where. We were very concerned about finding our way home. And in the meantime we were also half-starved, because earlier in Schweidnitz and also in Breslau they had only fed us out of a type of pig bucket. Even the feed in my pig bucket in Kauern was better! Here bread crusts swam in a white-colored broth, water with a little milk. In Warsaw, for the first time we got something to eat—a plate of warm noodles, which was of course wonderful. The Russian colonel had ordered that someone should take us to Breslau. A young Polish soldier was supposed to carry out the order. He was angry about it, for he had just come to Warsaw, where he wanted to stay; and now he was supposed to go back to Breslau! He decided to take his girlfriend along. The train stood about a kilometer outside the completely destroyed train station; the city looked devastated in general. The main street was full of mountains of rubble, and German prisoners of war were busy with the clean up. That was at the beginning of March 1946.

This Polish policeman who was supposed to take us captured "aristovani" to Breslau brought a load of suitcases along; he lugged baskets, bags, cartons. But *he* didn't lug them—Muto and I had to do it. And sometimes when we weren't fast enough for him, he flicked at our calves with his whip and said, "Davai, davai"—faster, faster. Since the train was standing fairly far from the destroyed train station, and we were rather weakened after these weeks and months, we had great difficulty carrying this stuff. I think he made us lug it because he was so angry that he had to make the trip again on account of us. Because the train connections were so bad, he would have to stay in Breslau again for the time being; he would not simply be able to travel back the next day.

By then we were standing in front of this train that was still empty, and we had set down all the suitcases. He ordered us to carry them all into the compartment. We tried that, but we couldn't do it because they were too heavy for us. I said, "I can't do it, they are too heavy for me." Then he said, "You Nazi pig." I thought, "That is going too far" and said, "That I am not." Then he slapped me and said again, "You Nazi pig." And I again, "No, I'm not." Slap. I got another one. But he did take the suitcases in himself, and then he led us into a second compartment, where we sat pressed very close to each other like turtle doves.

The train gradually filled up. A Russian man and a Russian

woman, both in uniform, sat down across from me. As on the trip there it was again uncomfortably close. Suddenly the Russian man said, "You German?" I nodded. He took a bottle of Schista vodka out of his pocket—that is an especially high-proof, good vodka—poured a water-glass full, gave it to me, and said, "Drink!" Then I said, "I haven't eaten anything proper in weeks, I'm afraid that I'll get drunk." "Drink!" he said seriously and severely, but not unfriendly.

Russians don't like it when they want to do something good for you and you refuse. So I took the vodka and drank it. He was absolutely right. It was as though with each swallow life, warmth, and a feeling of happiness came into me; once again I became warm and alive from the inside out. And he was happy to see that and finally pulled liverwurst sandwiches out of his pocket.

In that way we returned to Breslau. But not to freedom as we had hoped, but back to prison. On the highest floor in an ice cold cell where water dripped from the walls and where the only item was a little piece of mattress. There we had to stay three weeks. These weeks were really horrible, especially since the Russian colonel had said we would be free. We received food only irregularly and had the feeling they had forgotten us completely. I feared that no one knew any longer that there were still two people up there.

That was the only time when even Muto was really full of despair. But finally someone came and called us by some kind of name and said that we were now free. Upon leaving we received something to eat, then we went down the tall staircase out of the building and first sat down on the stone staircase of the prison. The sun was shining, it smelled like spring, and it was like a rebirth after all those weeks. Everything that had gone on before was not so bad—had been more civilized; but what we'd just experienced here in Breslau was a place where coldness and meanness permeated everything.

Now we were finally sitting in the sun and wondering what

to do! We decided to go to Caritas. At that time the director was an old gentleman to whom we told everything. However, by then the French consul (surprisingly, there was one in this city), commissioned by the Americans to look for us, had already approached him so that Caritas already knew about us. Freya Moltke had asked the Americans in Berlin to search for us, for she had no idea where we were. No one knew. We had been sorely missed, although at first they had thought we were running around in Silesia and were with friends. In any case, that's what the director of Caritas told us. No one had come upon the idea that we were sitting in jail. He made us some breakfast, and I recall that he climbed high up on a ladder in his library, brought out a bottle of wine from behind the books and said, "The Lord God did not forbid David to eat the display bread. He will also not forbid us to drink the communion wine."

But now what to do with us? It was clear that we could not so easily cross the Neisse again. Our protector therefore gave us over to the Catholic Saint George's hospital. It was run by a nun from Upper Silesia who could speak German as well as Polish and who had already during the war used Polish doctors as drafted assistant doctors in her hospital. At that time she had treated these doctors exactly like the German doctors, and now the assistants had become the Polish medical directors. But she reigned like a queen over everything. She was a magnificent woman with an extraordinary organizational talent and much warmth and steadfastness in her manner. When she went through the corridors of the big hospital in the mornings it was as though the captain was inspecting his ship. This woman took us under her wing, and we received a hospital room with two beds. Of course she had to do that secretly because the doctors could tolerate no foreign people in their hospital. One of her nurses, Sister Spiridia, first got busy cleaning us up, for we were as dirty as the hunting dogs we once owned! We got a hot bath and she combed our long hair, which was full of lice. But instead of then putting a chemical pack on our heads she began to really delouse us, like a mother monkey. She squashed each individual louse! While doing that she chattered lovingly and cheerfully, something we had done without for so long.

Sister Spiridia also had a close relationship to the remaining German population, which lived in fear and poverty. She knew women who bore children, men who returned from imprisonment, old people who were suffering; she knew exactly what was needed. And while the head nun kept the big sheets carefully in the big closets, Sister Spiridia would go there now and again, take one out, and make shirts out of it or diapers for the children. Of course she then got a reprimand from the head nun, but you noticed that the latter really thought it was completely in order. Sister Spiridia said, in this regard, "It is not hard for me to keep the vow of chastity, nor that of poverty, but with obedience, there's a problem!

In the process of relocating the convent to which the hospital belonged, we were also taken to Berlin. That was once again an adventurous trip. Caritas had asked us to carry messages, and so bound to our stomachs we had letters, news, reports, jewelry pieces. Of course, along with these there were also many political reports that Caritas in Breslau had received from Warsaw and that were supposed to be forwarded to Germany. The director of the transport was also an Upper Silesian who spoke Polish as well as German. In Küstrin the train stopped for a long time because of the border check, in the course of which they arrested and took away the director, precisely because she carried so many documents and things on her. The Poles had become distrustful. In any case, not until hours of waiting did the train finally head out again, and when it clattered over a temporary bridge across the Oder I said to Muto, "Who do you think will count the stones that are now falling from our hearts into the water?"

In Berlin someone from Caritas received us, and in the train station bathroom we handed over all the things. We then traveled alone in the S-Bahn, which at that time was already partially back in operation, back to Hortensienstrasse, where we were warmly welcomed by Maria and the others.

The wandering through Silesia, the complete escape from my old life and the beginning of a new one had given me strength and courage and a sense of adventure. I had not been broken by what had happened. In jail I had so firmly embedded Peter within me that I was full of life. But soon Muto became seriously ill. I often wondered if all this hadn't been too much for her—this walking and traveling through Silesia and the prison time. In any case, I did not feel threatened by the destruction of our old way of life. Sometimes I even think that I first learned to walk at the age of forty. Before that I was so fixed; my whole life played itself out only in connection with Peter—I lived only for him, through him, and I distanced myself further from my own family. This new life began in the Berlin prison. In the time between the Twentieth of July and the beginning of October, when I got out of prison, I went through a transformation. Everything I had experienced seemed to have been worked through in jail. It was as though I first had to search for myself and then I actually found myself. The prison and the time with Muto in Silesia helped me and molded me. But somehow Peter was always there; so much so that I sometimes thought he was shut up inside me as if by a metamorphosis. . . .

But now the question presented itself as to how Muto and I were supposed to find our way back to a middle-class existence. Of course Muto was a trained doctor, and she had periodically practiced in Silesia; for a while she directed the Wansener Hospital. She knew that she would immediately find work again. She went to the Auguste-Viktoria-Hospital in Schöneberg and became an assistant doctor there. Later she had her own practice as an internist. Her teacher was Viktor von Weizsäcker, the founder of anthropological medicine.

With me everything was much more difficult. I had the first

law exam and a doctorate of law, but I was still lacking the licensing exam, the practice, and the confidence: in short, the job experience, because for ten years I'd been concerned almost exclusively with farming. While I was still racking my brains about this, Raddatz the Communist came to see me one day, and on behalf of Wilhelm Pieck (later the President of the DDR) offered me a position in municipal government. Berlin was not yet divided, so there was only one municipal government. I told them I had never worked in an office before, because they had immediately offered me a department in the main office for social affairs, which was run at that time by a Communist by the name of Ottomar Geschke.

So I started out in city hall and was warmly received. One of my coworkers was Anna Rehme, formerly the secretary to Clara Zetkin, a courageous Communist. The work went very well. I had to look after victims of persecution and their survivors. Families that had been torn apart were brought back together, and I secured living space for them and so on, but most of all I kept busy just finding the people in the first place.

In the fall of 1946 there was a celebration in honor of the victims of fascism. I was supposed to make a speech, along with Robert Havemann and Greta Kuckhoff. Her husband was a physicist who had been killed by the Nazis in a concentration camp. Havemann had spent years in the Brandenburg prison together with Erich Honecker. Later he was also persecuted by the SED. I had prepared a speech, in my opinion well and carefully, but like the others it had to be submitted to a Russian colonel for inspection. He objected to the conclusion, a Gorky quotation. He said, "Everything is good, but not Gorky." I said, "But it has to have a conclusion, and preferably a poetic conclusion and not a political one." He no doubt recognized that, and I gave the speech and concluded, thinking of my husband and my friends, with the words: "The idea for which our husbands died is our precious legacy. For them Gorky's words from "The Falcon" hold true:

Though you are dead,
in the song of the brave and those strong in spirit
you live as an example, as a proud call
to light and freedom.

But back to everyday life. The Americans were very friendly to us. Again and again someone came by and brought us either grapefruit or gigantic loaves of white bread, and we had grocery ration coupons in abundance, because as victims of persecution we received more, and because about twenty-five people were officially registered at Hortensienstrasse. They came here from everywhere, from Mecklenburg, Silesia, Pomerania, and then stayed a while. Freya was registered with us, as were many nieces and nephews. Maria heard more than once, "The Countess does not need to take quite so many people in with her! After all, she has a right to this house."

We always had enough to eat. Once an English soldier rang at the door. I opened it, and there he stood with a whole pile of wool blankets over his arm and asked me, "Are you Marion?" "Yes," I said. "Take it," he replied, and he was gone. I also received a lot of CARE packages, which I usually passed on to families with children.

A close solidarity developed immediately among the women of the resistance: Freya Moltke, Barbara Haeften, Clarita Trott, Annedore Leber, Romai Reichwein, Käthe Jessen, Mrs. Olbricht, Mrs. Hoepner. We met each other often, and we helped each other. The connection was so close that some of our children even married each other.

Professionally, it turned out different for me than I had imagined. Gradually I came to realize that I was somehow being used by the Communist government. Sometimes I felt pushed and steered, without knowing by whom or in what direction. Gradually I noticed that I was supposed to become a bourgeois show piece for the Communists. The classless society, which after the war had developed very beneficially in Berlin, so that everyone was really involved with everyone else, had soon crystallized into groups and classes and parties. The SED had already been founded; Social Democrats and Communists had joined together, partially voluntarily, partially forced, in the Soviet Occupied Zone and the corresponding sector of Berlin. Berlin was not yet divided; there were only the sectors of the victorious powers, and for that reason the Social Democrats kept their independence in the three West sectors. In any case I thought that it was probably better as a woman to have a learned profession with which I could represent myself clearly, firmly, and without party politics. For I had the same feeling as other women: in the end you were only a kind of social entity, highly courted, but always passed around. That was not pleasant. You were certainly important, but had no influence whatsoever.

I then consulted with Ulrich Biel, whom I had met in the last days of March of 1946. He was a political advisor to the American commander Howley and had also come to our house through his friend Paulus van Husen—one of the very few survivors of the Twentieth of July. Our friendship began at that time, developing eventually into the almost forty year long relationship we have today. Ulrich had to emigrate in 1934 to the United States and had actively participated in the war. He quickly fascinated me with his directness and with his intelligence. He had lost all of his family members in a concentration camp. We understood one another right away, and so it has remained up to the present day. Through him I have gained a lively relationship to politics and to public life in general. Since freedom has arrived we have learned and experienced much more of the world than was possible up to 1945. So Ulrich advised me, "You know, you should take the licensing exam." I had reservations at first because I no longer remembered anything from my studies. Above all, I did not really think I could do it. Furthermore, in Berlin there was still no testing office for the exam. So I went to Hilde Benjamin. At that time she directed the main office for judicial affairs in Berlin, which was not yet divided, and I discussed with her how I wanted to go again through a phase as a law clerk and then register for the licensing exam. Hilde Benjamin, with whom I had a good conversation, was very taken with the idea. She was a clever person and a good jurist; her husband had lost his life in a concentration camp. At that time she was not as much a fanatic Communist as later. She wore her hair in a fat bun and was not unlikable. So we spoke with one another, and when I had said goodbye and was already standing at the door, she said at the end and in an offhand way, "In Potsdam we already have a main testing office—you can take your exam there." I said, "Potsdam?" "Yes," she replied. "Of course you would have to take up residence there." "Oh," I said. "I'll think about that." And when I came home I thought, "I have lived in this dear house with Peter, it is like a snail shell, why should I move to Potsdam?" At that time a good spirit kept me from becoming a People's Judge in Potsdam. Later, the Russians tried once again to lure me over. A colonel called me several times and said I should come and talk about the Kreisauers. I would be picked up and brought back home. But I declined.

So I waited until there was a main testing office in the West part of Berlin and wrote that to Hilde Benjamin. I never saw her again. She later became the chief prosecutor of the DDR.

I then registered for a law clerk position at the local court in Lichterfelde, only ten minutes away from Hortensienstrasse. However, because the Justice Department had hardly any judges untainted by the past, I very quickly became an acting judge, while I was still a law clerk. During this time I had to decide civil as well as criminal cases. I worked very hard in those days. These judgments, which I could confidently sign with Yorck, often kept me in the libraries. Ulrich helped me a lot with them. So I was an acting judge. Also, at that time I often participated with interest in the proceedings of the American court; Judge Sabo was a model of judicial independence for me.

Of course, I was often asked about people who had played a role in the Third Reich. I helped many with de-nazification, but when I didn't know anything I also said, "I know nothing, this person's life history is unknown to me." Therefore, my certificates were valuable: they were not whitewashes.

Then in the fall of 1947 a main testing office was established in the old Berlin Regional Court, near Alexanderplatz. I knew that the first tests were to take place in November, so I gathered my courage and registered, after I had already been active not only in Lichterfelde, but also in the newly established regional court in Zehlendorf. I learned a lot from the judge who presided there. Then, at forty-three years of age, I sat myself down, did my homework for the licensing exam, and passed it. I first became an associate in a civil chamber—again with a good presiding judge, who once gave me the advice, "Whatever you issue, a decision or a judgement, there must be *one* idea in it. No more and no less. . . ." And I remembered that well.

The other associate in this chamber was the future Superior Court of Justice president von Drenkmann, who was murdered in 1974 by terrorists. One day I was ordered to see the Regional Court president, who announced to me that he wanted to have me as an associate in a criminal court in Moabit, for the occupying powers understandably insisted on criminal judges who were completely untainted by their political past.

I had only been a criminal judge for a short time! But I had adjusted well in this civil court personally and in terms of the law. So I said, "That doesn't suit me." To that the Regional Court president said, "If you don't want to, we could say you might get a crying fit, then I would have a good reason not to insist." I answered, "Oh, I have never had such a thing!"

And so I became a criminal judge in Moabit, and I sometimes caused the administration difficulties, because I had my own way of carrying out the trials and of treating the defendants and prisoners, their families, the witnesses, and all these people, rather than using the usual officialese. Consequently, several times they offered me another position at the Superior Court of Justice, at the Federal Court or with the Senator for Justice, but

I said, "Now I'm staying in Moabit." And by then I also presided in a Grand Juvenile Criminal Court; I kept that position almost twenty years. In 1952 I also became the first woman to preside over a jury court.

I was, by the way, considered a strict judge. But I always tried to do justice to both humanity and to the judicial office. I still remember that once at the conclusion of an opinion I said, "I am the victim's last resort." After the crime, the psychologist and educators come immediately—I was working in juvenile criminal law—to investigate and save the defendant. But the victim is no longer the concern of anybody, except perhaps the parents.

The postwar period also produced its own cases. I still recall a criminal case before a jury. Two black market gangs in the area of Kurfürstendamm fought each other bitterly. Once it came to a shootout and to a criminal proceeding against one participant because of attempted murder. The main defendant was called Kurzbart. A Jew, he had survived in the Warsaw ghetto and later in the underground in an adventurous way. He was successful in delaying the trial eight times because there was no interpreter in the right language; he understood my German immediately, and we negotiated without language difficulties. I gave him the legal advice that he could also be convicted of attempted *manslaughter*, because he was not ready to disclose any motive. On the second day of the trial the Superior Court of Justice president had come to listen in on me. My way of carrying out a trial bothered him; he was absolutely against women in judicial matters, and he had already tried several times to catapult me out of my criminal court. But he had not been successful, and now he was there to listen in on me. However, he did not sit down as usual in front of me in the courtroom, but rather diagonally behind me. When I gave the defendant this legal advice the president cleared his throat loudly. I took no notice of it, but rather carried out the trial to the end, and the man was sentenced to "only" eight years of jail because of attempted manslaughter. But afterwards when I was in my judge's chamber the defense lawyer came to me and said, "The defendant told me: 'The woman was decent to me, so I'll be decent to her. I accept the decision.'"

Now that was still at a time when many judges had an understandable fear of sentencing Jewish defendants. In the ensuing opinion I added that a German judge could hardly dare to require law-abiding behavior from these people, after everything that they suffered from the Germans. But the Superior Court of Justice President did not find all that proper: he wanted to see the defendant sentenced for attempted murder.

In 1950, in a jury court, I sat as an associate judge with an old colleague—with Korsch, a good and somewhat impatient judge, from whom I learned a lot, and a level-headed and benevolent man. I recall there a case that was cruelly typical of the postwar period. They had found body parts of two dead people in the ruins. Ruins generally were favorite hiding places. The things that were found there! The whole thing came to light because a child had come home and said, "Mama, today I found a roast for us in the ruins." The criminal police in the East and the West searched and searched and had no clues whatsoever. They were able only to figure out from missing person reports who those dead people were. The police and the experts were of the opinion: It can only have been a doctor or a butcher, no other person can so expertly carve up a corpse. Finally they came up with an operating room nurse from the Robert-Koch-Hospital, who had written a postcard to one of the victims. She had killed two people because she wanted to give her lover presents and didn't have enough money. She was a pretty woman with an excessive need for admiration. The case occupied the imagination of Berliners, as, in general, human destinies in Moabit often moved Berliners in those postwar years.

The two decades of my work as a criminal judge helped me to understand human faults and errors and to do them justice. I was constantly endeavoring not to let my work become routine and to practice the judicial office without arrogance.

Well, for almost forty years I've been living here in Berlin to-gether with Ulrich and Maria. In a nice home, with a garden, into which I settle more and more! Through Ulrich—unlike my life before 1945—I have met many leading foreign and German politicians; already by 1945 he had held long conversations with Adenauer, and during the Berlin Blockade Ernst Reuter came al-most every day to have breakfast with him. Reuter had a good sense of humor and was similar to Leber, even in his physical ap-pearance. He was a heavy man, walked with a cane, and wore a beret. He came from Friesland, was first a Social Democrat, then for a short time a Communist; later in 1947 he became the Social Democrat mayor of Berlin against the opposition of the Russians. He died in 1953.

A year previously, Ulrich had renewed his German citizen-ship and had become a lawyer like his father, and for many years he was an elected representative in Berlin.

Finally, I could write a whole book about Maria. We've been living together for more than fifty years now, and she is the most important bridge between my earlier and my present life. She shared all the worries with us, with Peter and me; she also knew at that time what was going on, and she acted level headed and shrewd during the interrogations by the Gestapo. After the as-sassination attempt she was drafted to work in a hospital in Wannsee and from there was evacuated with the wounded in a venturesome convoy from the Havel to the Elbe. But in De-cember 1945 she came over the Green Zone border back to Hortensienstrasse. I cannot imagine my life without Maria and her warmth, inner confidence, and cheerfulness. For me she was always like a mother, sister, and best friend.

And last of all, the few letters that I still possess from Peter have accompanied me all these years. The letter was his favorite medium. He did not speak much; he preferred to write. And he wrote me even during our briefest separations. Sometimes, when he had to leave early I found a letter on the nightstand or on the pillow. He had to tell me everything: the details of his daily routine, his momentary problems, whom he saw and to whom he spoke, what plans he had, how he felt, which shrubs or flowers were blooming in the garden—simply everything. But he was especially occupied with the details of Kauern and of farming, above all with the big garden in Kauern and the small one at Hortensienstrasse. I hesitated for a long time to give his letters over to the public because they really seemed only meant for me, but in the context of a story like this one, it wouldn't be complete without them.

I am, by the way, happy to be getting old and find life as an old person actually easier than as a young person, because like in the theater you are sitting in the first or second circle. You look at life. Sometimes you are surprised, sometimes you have worries. You live more through your being than through your actions. I think that as a young person life is at times very strenuous. First of all, it is strenuous to be in love. Then it is strenuous to choose a profession for oneself. And finally it is strenuous to understand the consequences of one's actions and that one must accept them. In spite of that, I wouldn't want to do without the dangers and the sorrows of my life. It could be that only someone who has survived them so well and who enjoys living as much as I do can say such a thing. For that I am thankful.

Peter Yorck's Letters to His Wife

[Summer 1943; Berlin]

My most beloved Sunday child,

What a difference between today and a week ago. No longer the togetherness, filled with closeness, pervaded with love, as celebrated so beautifully in Solomon's Song of Songs, including even the two fawns, but rather a quiet and proper Sunday, solitary but not resigned. I am always being reproached for philosophical composure; I don't think that this reproach is correct. It is rather the humble recognition of my own powerlessness and the vital desire to be able to place everything in God's hand with confidence and peace. Lilje's sermon today was a real encouragement to do that; the hymns that preceded it and those that followed it were all hymns of praise, and that was also the theme of the sermon. It was devoted to Psalm 118 as a whole and in particular to verse 17: "I shall not die, but I shall live, and recount the deeds of the Lord." This is the verse that Luther wrote on the wall of Coburg castle and that stands at the beginning of Saint Augustine's *Confessions*. When Lilje himself was seeking comfort during the World War he applied it to himself, and now he applied it primarily to the followers of Christ and to the church, and he organized it as follows: 1. Experienced faith increases inner peace and confidence. 2. Out of experienced faith grows a new feeling of God's presence.—After lunch I spoke with Hans Haeften about church affairs. The Michaels brothers, of course, have a particular opinion about the organization of church service, especially the liturgy and the Communion celebration. They have high hopes that, among other things, a richer service will more easily bring back those who are estranged from the church. When you think of the many weak sermons that are given in Protestant churches, you can't help wondering whether this matter of concern is not justified. For it would address and satisfy the mystical part of the religious feeling, whereas the proclamation of the word is based only on the sermon, and a weak sermon does not reach the person who is searching and does not become the gate of the Lord through which he would enter. The reason these questions have become so problematic can probably be traced back to the fact that spiritual and religious substance have not grown at the same rate as did the population. That even this blanket is too short. I feel more and more powerless before this task that must be accomplished, and for that reason I very much needed your guiding and uplifting words of encouragement. It is a very nice prospect that this is to be granted to me as early as the day after tomorrow.

Greetings, God bless you

Peter

[Probably the end of December 1943; Berlin]

Dearest Tuschelchen,

In glancing in the DAZ I had to think especially of you, for there was the headline: "Beethoven in Ceremonial Taps," and the text explained that from now on the hymn "I Pray to the Power of Love,"[1] would be replaced by the hymn "Praise the Heavens."[2] As the fifth year of the war comes to a close one can certainly see why it is so urgent to order such a change. Because at the present time love has disappeared from the world to such a degree that the adoration of its power would seem to be daring. Furthermore, it is the revelation of the love in Jesus that this hymn celebrates. This is a far cry from the Second Silesian War and the Battle of Kesselsdorf where the old Dessauer began his order to attack with "Forward in the Name of Jesus!" The changing course of the world in these two centuries is quite well illustrated by these two episodes, and yet, even the soldier of our time, in unison with the heavens, has reason not only to praise the honor of the Eternal, but also to adore the power of love,

1. "Ich bete an die Macht der Liebe."

2. "Die Himmel rühmen." Beethoven, "Six Songs," No. 4, Opus 48.

whose banishment from the world pronounces judgement upon the world. And where shall we find a more perfect revelation of love than in the figure of Jesus Christ?—Who will take note of this change? Who will grasp its meaning and significance and take an appropriate stand?—Yesterday evening was quite nice. Ernst [Siemens] has really matured after all, and the lone wolf has become a family and company member, who consciously pursues his goals with firmness and energy. It is curious how important his father has become to him. In his youth the contrast of their personalities appeared so strong that, as an outsider, you did not have the impression that they were extremely close. Today when he makes reference to his father it is always with approval, even admiration. The son has gained greatly by this and has fashioned for himself a point of orientation and an anchor, which certainly serves him well. From his stories it became evident how great a conflict there is for the businessman who is also a public servant. At some point this question will have to be more thoroughly discussed.—I hope you had a good trip, met Heimeran [?] and had a successful discussion [re: vegetable drying kiln]. You should also discuss with him the matter concerning the optimal size of the installation. You certainly discussed the [?] I suggested and also the orchard. With very special thoughts I am with you today and kiss your hand.

Peter

[Probably May 1944; after communion with Lilje]

My wife whom I love more and more profoundly,

You still haven't left Berlin and the Adieu or, in German the *Gott befohlen* (God bless you), still sounds in my ear and burns in my heart. But this pain is cooled by a surge of thankfulness for such a day in the middle of such a time. I feel moved in a special way and sometimes it seems to me as though new strength grows out of all that has happened. Of course, very soon doubt makes its presence felt: the question, whether this is not just an optimistic illusion. In the face of such days as yesterday, however, this doubt cannot prevail; it is an effective force. The intensity of the experience has increased for many people, and therefore, yesterday morning one could feel such a compressed and concentrated feeling among those involved. All individual events and individual impressions are compressed into the awareness of the ruling destiny, and the omnipotence of God becomes, so to speak, a palpable and overpowering influence in this world. It is remarkable that next to the feeling of being threatened, the feeling of being turned upside down and the instability of the moment, there exists a hope full of trust, and the feeling of being called is stronger than the feeling of being judged. In this sense, yesterday's celebration bestowed on me a graceful strength, and I felt myself driven in a special way to participate in it. In the mutuality of this experience there also lies a special gift, and that remains intact, even though we are temporarily separated. Because the continuity of country life, this becoming and growing and developing, bears a very lively correlation to my life here, which has to be lived disjointedly without predictability and foundation and could easily lack a firm footing. For through you and with you Kauern is in fact much closer and much more alive and strengthening rather than burdensome. Otherwise Hans might sometimes cast a reproachful look, and a vacuum could develop that would be difficult to bridge. These days, the hearts of the people are wide open and even in need (which means you must speak with them and share their troubles). In giving to them you gain strength yourself. And so at the moment you are gathering more strength there than would be possible here and are making me happy with your letters, thoughts, and with such beautiful days as the last two. Certainly this is no permanent life, but then our present condition cannot be permanent either. It contradicts the laws of nature and the order of the creator.—And so today in my heart there is only gratitude and confidence and love for my wife beyond expression. God be with you. Very affectionate hand kiss,

Peter

[Very likely 23 July 1944; Ravensbrück Concentration Camp]

My dear wife,

In celebration of Sunday they have kindly given me an ink pen and paper so that I can write you. You have certainly already gotten news from Lottchen [the sister of Siemens]. So you know where I am. Since I don't know whether it is allowed I will write nothing about the reason and circumstances of my being here. I hope that my mishap gets cleared up and that thereby you will be free of one worry. Please also tell dear Mother that I am very sad to cause her this worry in addition to the pain of her two fallen sons. She should not get upset, that is not good for her heart. — You can imagine how shaken I am by this event and how much it occupies me during these long days. For in contrast to the Berlin day, here you concretely feel the truth of Goethe: "The hour has one hundred minutes, the day has more than a thousand."[3] As soon as I have books, I'll make use of this. Presently, all that's left to me is pure meditation. I didn't specify the books I wanted and would like to do that now: I would like the Bible, Holl—the first volume is in the office—Uncle Max's World History, books on agriculture—these are also in the office. From there I would also like my fountain pen. I had asked there for information about the public theater schedule and for theater tickets for the coming week; please cancel these. I would like a deck of cards to play solitaire. For the moment I've fabricated myself a set out of toilet paper. I need a mirror for shaving. Shoe shining items, sewing thread, and a dark uniform but-

---

3. Peter Yorck mistakenly quotes Goethe as saying that the hour has one hundred, instead of sixty minutes. The quotation in its entirety can be found in the Weimar Edition of Goethe's Works, vol. I, 4, p. 267:

> Ihrer sechzig hat die Stunde,
> über Tausend hat der Tag.
> Söhnchen! werde dir die Kunde,
> was man alles leisten mag.

It is Goethe's advice about making the most of all the minutes of the day.

ton. Also letter-writing paper and postage. Then please subscribe to the VB [*Völkischer Beobachter*] for me, otherwise one is cut off too much from world and war events.—I am egotistically writing only about myself, but can assure you that I am thinking very lovingly of you and of all the additional burden that is on you now. But please take care of Tischer's building matter, the threshing machine and Fischer's other machines, and the progress of the field train. As soon as the ordering and fertilizer plan is complete after you've discussed it with Görbing and you receive permission to talk, we have to discuss it. In addition I have to give you bank authority for Delbrück and Eichborn [banks]. Please send the necessary forms. Are you taking Marie-chen to Kauern? Please make sure that for the time being no appointments are scheduled in the arbitration court matter. Yesterday a bad storm and hail came down here—that surely caused a lot of damage. Hopefully the harvest will go smoothly with us. I am not allowed to write any more, but I am allowed to think of you every hour. And so I am with you with strong and loving feelings.

I tenderly kiss your hands,

Peter

[7 and 8 August 1944, before the sentence]

Dearly beloved child of my heart,

We are probably standing at the end of our beautiful and rich life together. Because tomorrow the People's Court intends to sit in judgment on me and others. I hear that we have been expelled from the army. They can take the uniform from us, but not the spirit in which we acted. And in that I feel united with our fathers and brothers and comrades.

The fact that God ordained what has happened is part of his fathomless decrees, which I humbly accept. I believe myself to be pure of heart yet driven by the feeling of guilt that weighs on all of us. I therefore also confidently hope that I find a merciful judge in God.

You, my wife whom I love above all else, I leave behind in a very dark world with fervent prayers for your protection. When we went home from the last communion I had an almost eerie feeling of elevation—I would like to call it nearness to Christ. Looking back, it seems to me that it was a call. It was so beautiful, this life with you, always upward bound in spite of all the pain that we experienced in it. I felt so richly showered with gifts by your love; my gratitude is great beyond expression. I also see a grace in that I was not called away sooner. For I know, today I won't leave you behind without roots. Today you have a home to which you are anchored with a thousand threads of love. Just as I know you to be secure there, so I place the welfare and woe of Kauern into your hands with complete trust. You earned it for yourself in these last years. Now own it and fill it with your human beauty. Don't consider this task to be too difficult. Love makes it easy and worth living. You have sown love and love you will reap; also that which Hans sprinkled in and what I endeavored to increase to the best of my ability, will grow for you.

Even though I am going away from here, my brave one, I am not leaving you alone. Wherever you go, my love, my caring thoughts, my prayers will accompany you. During these sixteen long days I have been picturing your life as if I were part of it. The extension of the upper story to the granary stairs, on the right two additional big rooms, of which the one in back would have two windows and be decorated with the Berlin living room furniture, and the dish closet on the right becomes a bathroom.

I saw the big garden, and in it Mariechen as the wife of a gardener to be engaged. Instead of the shrub border in the present garden, I saw, on the right and left toward the front, rose borders with green onions, retaining the middle path but edged only with long-stemmed roses as a flower border. I saw the bench and the starter beds, the second half of them early beds and behind them one or two hot houses, where one could perhaps move the wall forward by the width of the barn or even up to the corner. I saw Reichert Wilhelm, after his training at the riding and driving school, grandly on the coach box, and my uniform reworked into carriage liveries gave him the grand appearance that he must have as the coachman of the most gracious, most capable countess. I saw the big garden sensibly divided by means of fruit shrubs and flowers, nothing embellished, but also no plantation either. I saw the abundant fruit blossoms outside and the beautiful harvest, but also the cattle on the well irrigated pasture near the row of houses at Kauern or on the Lorzendorfer meadow. It was a picture of the fruitful activity of love, on which my eyes feasted.

My dearest little heart, I want to continue to participate in everything, and I see that Goldchen and my sisters keep taking loving care of you. Bia too will be caring and helpful, and so I may be at peace and close my life with deep gratitude. We will, of course, still see each other; then we don't want to be just sad that it's all over, but rather be full of thanks that it was so beautiful and will remain unforgettably beautiful. Perhaps Herr Lilje will be so kind as to come to the house and say some last words, and also hold a quiet prayer service at Kauern.

Look for a place for both us where we can be very near each other. And the memorial stone for Hans, make it for us three: for Hans who lived and worked; for Heinrich, who made a generous sacrifice; and for Peter, who continued to build. Then all three of us will always be there.

Now they want to shut me down, as it's called here. So good night, I entrust you to God's goodness and ask him for strength. I very tenderly kiss your hands,

Your Peter

Apparently they are in a hurry to carry out the sentence. For that reason we have the opportunity to write once again even before the pronouncement of the verdict. Whether you will be successful in seeing me once more appears to me rather doubtful. Therefore, dearest wife, I would like to talk with you this very hour and continue our dialogue.

In order to relieve you of business matters, especially the matters which concern the confiscation of the property, I gave Bia a detailed list. It will be easier for him to carry out these negotiations. Since he is, of course, the owner of Kauern [Peter Yorck made this comment with reference to the impending property confiscation] I suggested to him to lease it to you. As concerns the lease, in my opinion, consideration needs to be given to the payments for Goldchen and my sisters, and further, to the interest and amortization of the sum that Bia is paying out of his own pocket in order to pay for the property forfeited by the confiscation. Please tell him that, for I omitted to write him about it. For me it would be a great comfort to know that you were at Kauern. I would quickly give the Berlin apartment to friends, and starting the first of September pay no more rent. Perhaps Freya [Moltke] or Brigitte [Gerstenmaier] would be interested in it. It would be best for you to take your furniture and so forth to Kauern; perhaps Herr Joesch with the state railway administration can be of help. You are now so alone in this difficult life, my Tuschelchen. But I know your courage and love, and I will continue to stand by you, you can be sure of that.

But now I want to think of the many loved ones to whom you must please give my regards. How shall I repay all the love I received from them? Tell Tekchen [Irene Yorck], above all, that I'm really counting on her to look after you with great care. Tell her she should move her practice to Kauern and live with you. In doing so she will profit just as much or more than you, and she knows that too. Dävchen must now do without my humble advice. But tell her, she should try it with [Inspector] Wagner for only one year. If it does not work out, then she has got to change. Considering Wagner's age she should not wait. Unfortunately I didn't speak with the Tiergarten tax office. I wish her and her children all the best, as well as the other sisters. I can no longer individualize my greetings, wishes and pleas.

And now I come to our friends. The fact that my visit at Sylvius's [Pückler] turned out to be my swan song has moved me curiously. It further amuses me that Ulla [Mangoldt] has not been heard from at all. You must give my warm greetings to that old rascal [Luckner]. Perhaps he can use some of my suits or underwear and will paint you a picture of me as the unlucky rebel for freedom, human dignity, and justice. He was so unhappy with me, but I hope he will forgive me. Very warm greetings to little Kling [coworker]. Give him my Lassalle Heraklit; I hope he won't get into trouble on my account. Teddy [Kessel], Gogo [Nostitz], and the many others, Reyali [Freya Moltke], Helmuth and whoever else there is, Paulus and Lukas [Lukaschek], to them my regards and my thanks. How could I in this hour think of everything that they and their friendship have meant to us! Mariechen will certainly not leave you. She should pray for me and keep me in loving memory. She knows, of course, how I love her and how grateful I am to her.

In Kauern you must, of course, tell each person with what happiness and gratitude I think of everyone, how I share their concern about the people away from home and how much I wish them all a speedy peace. Please don't leave them, they need you very much, and their trust and their love will also support you. Good [Inspector] Lampl now experiences it again for the second time. Give him a memento from me, perhaps Diter's silver box or Koljas's cuff links. Assure him of my deep gratitude and trust. He will certainly not go away so soon and will stand by your side.

Give my godchildren mementos, like my watch to Tiechen, the Abeken to Gebchen, the Heter clock to Peter Voss, the shotgun that is in Kleinöls perhaps later to the little Schulenburg and the Frederick the Great to little Katte. It is difficult to find a gift for the two nieces. Also my regards to your brothers and sisters. Abs, Borsig, and all the others will always be there for you. Don't let those ties be broken, which have so greatly enriched our life. Invite our friends over and don't forget the ones from East Prussia in doing so. Keep the richness in your life; it is so infinitely gratifying to receive and to give love. The greatest wish of my heart is that my death will reestablish harmony with Bia. Please also do your part in this regard. For him too it will be a new opportunity.

Now it proves to be fortunate that I inherited neither Kleinöls nor Kauern [see p. 89] and that, therefore, they are both not in danger. With the arbitrator and the lawyer you will certainly come to terms about the payment or reimbursement; it is to be deducted from the confiscated estate, of course, and is to be paid from it to start with.

But enough of these worries. Full of confidence, I entrust your future to God's goodness and to the love of my loved ones and yours. Our togetherness will continue, my dearest, even if my large hands can no longer caress you. In their place my thoughts will do that, and they will constantly surround and hover around you. My death will hopefully be accepted as atonement for all my sins and as a sacrifice for what we all bear in common. May my death contribute just a little to reduce our present day's distance from God. I also, for my part, die a death for the Fatherland. Though the outer appearance is inglorious, even ignominious, I go upright and unbowed on this last walk, and I hope that you do not see this as arrogance and delusion, but rather as someone who was faithful to the end! "We wanted to light the torch of life, a sea of flames surrounds us, what a fire!"

And now, for the last time, I say to you farewell. Be brave and strong, give love and have faith in love. Accept the inexpressibly profound gratitude of your husband who owes you the beauty of his life. My last prayer is that I commend you to God and ask for forgiveness for my sins and the salvation of my soul.

In the tender love, in which I lived with you here, I will continue to live. I hug you and caress and kiss your sweet hands,

Your husband

Glossary of Terms and Names

Avus. Abbreviation for *Autorennstrecke-Verkehrs-und Übungs-strasse*, a road that was originally used for test runs with race cars and new car models, as well as for car racing. It was later considered the first Autobahn in Germany when it was opened for normal traffic.

Caritas. Caritasverband, a Catholic charity organization.

DAZ. *Deutsche Allgemeine Zeitung*, a German newspaper.

DDR. *Deutsche Demokratische Republik* (the German Democratic Republic, or GDR), the official name of former East Germany.

Delp, Alfred, S. J. A Bavarian Jesuit active in the Kreisau Circle. Executed 2 February 1945.

de-nazification. Outlined in the Potsdam Agreement after the war, the goal of de-nazification was to purge Germany of all those who had supported Hitler. These people were to be removed from positions of power and punished. All institutions were to be led by people with no past Nazi affiliations.

Ehrensberger, Otto. A civil servant who knew and associated with members of the Kreisau Circle. However, he does not appear on the list of members of the conspiracy.

"Fontane's *Stechlin*." Theodor Fontane (1819–98) was a journalist and novelist from Brandenburg and Berlin. His popular novels, including *Der Stechlin*, contain many descriptions of the beautiful Prussian countryside in his native Brandenburg.

Freisler, Roland. A notorious judge who presided over the Nazi People's Court and sentenced many to death, including the participants in the 20 July 1944 conspiracy. Killed in an air raid on Berlin in February 1945.

Gauleiter. A leader of a Nazi administrative district.

Gerstenmaier, Eugen. An official of the German Evangelical

Church's Foreign Bureau and one of the few members of the Kreisau Circle to survive.

Gestapo. Nazi secret police.

Grunewald. The name of a district and a park in Berlin.

Haeften, Hans-Bernd von. A diplomat and leading member of the Kreisau Circle. Executed 15 August 1944.

Haubach, Theo. A journalist and member of the Kreisau Circle. Executed on 23 January 1945.

Havel. A tributary of the Elbe River, the Havel is joined by the Spree in Berlin. It is part of a system of canals linking the Elbe in the west to the Oder in the east.

Im Dol. The name of a street in Berlin.

Kessel, Albrecht von. A diplomat in the foreign service and friend of Adam von Trott zu Solz. He was not directly involved with the conspiracy to assassinate Hitler, but he was part of the resistance in the foreign ministry.

"Kortner's *Richard III*." Fritz Kortner was an actor in Weimar Germany who starred in plays produced by Leopold Jessner. These plays, including *Richard III*, often satirized the current political situation.

Kristallnacht. Also known as "night of the broken glass," which occurred during the night of 9–10 November 1938. Hitler's Storm Troopers and mobs of Germans burned and destroyed Jewish homes, synagogues, and businesses. Many Jews were killed during the night or rounded up and sent to concentration camps the next day.

Leber, Julius. A leading Social Democrat who was to head the new government after Hitler was removed. Executed 5 January 1945.

"Lessing's Nathan." German dramatist and critic Gotthold Ephraim Lessing (1729–81) wrote the first important plays in German. Nathan, a wise and truthful Jew who embodies Lessing's ideal of humanity, is a character in Lessing's *Nathan der Weise* (1779).

Mierendorff, Carlo. A Social Democrat and member of the Kreisau Circle. He was an important spiritual leader of the resistance. Killed in an air raid on Leipzig 4 December 1943.

Moabit. A district of Berlin and the site of the city's main jail.

Moltke, Helmuth James, Count von. A lawyer and advisor on military and international law. He was co-director of the Kreisau Circle with Peter Yorck. He was arrested 19 January 1944 for matters not having to do with the conspiracy. Executed 23 January 1945.

Neisse River. Together with the Oder, this river forms the boundary between Germany and Poland.

OKW. *Oberkommando der Wehrmacht*, the High Command of the Armed Forces.

Oberpräsidium. The provincial governor.

Oder River. *See* Neisse River.

People's Court. The name of the Nazi court, established in 1934.

Reinhardt, Max (1873–1943). A theatrical director famous for his innovative productions in Berlin in the early twentieth century.

Reichwein, Adolf. A professor, leading Social Democrat, and member of the Kreisau Circle. Executed 20 October 1944.

Röhm Putsch. Ernst Röhm was the leader of the SA. He and other SA members, along with various enemies of the regime, were executed by the SS on 30 June 1934. Hitler believed that the SA was becoming too powerful and was playing too large a role in political matters.

SA. *Sturmabteilung* (Storm Troopers), the Nazi paramilitary organization.

S-Bahn. *Stadtbahn*, the city railroad.

Schinkelbau. A building designed by the Berlin architect Karl Friedrich Schinkel (1781–1841).

Schmidt, Helmut. A Social Democrat and popular chancellor of West Germany from 1974 until 1982. He was succeeded by Helmut Kohl.

Schulenburg, Fritz-Dietlof, Count von der. A colonel who was one of the leading members of the military resistance. Executed 10 August 1944.

Schwerin von Schwanenfeld, Ulrich Wilhelm, Count von. An officer who served as a liaison between military and civilian resistance groups. Executed 8 September 1944.

SED. *Sozialistische Einheitspartei Deutschlands* (Socialist Unity Party of Germany), created by the more or less forced absorption of the Socialist Party into the Communist Party.

"Mrs. Solf's group." Another resistance group in Germany.

SS. *Schutzstaffel*, Hitler's personal guard.

Stauffenberg, Claus Schenk, Count von. A leader of the military conspiracy against Hitler. He carried out the assassination attempt on 20 July 1944 and was executed close to midnight the same day. Peter Yorck was his cousin.

"Stefan George circle." A literary group founded by Stefan George (1868–1933), a German lyric poet. Well-known writers were members of his circle or published in his journal. The Stauffenberg brothers were among its young, idealistic members. Stefan George rejected Nazism, although often his ideals, such as love of the fatherland, are considered similar to those of the Nazis.

Trott zu Solz, Adam von. A diplomat and member of the Kreisau Circle. Executed 26 August 1944.

Völkischer Beobachter. The official newspaper of the Nazi party.